the girls' guide to
GUYS

the girls' guide to
GUYS

Straight Talk on Flirting,
Dating, Breaking Up, Making Up,
and Finding True Love

Julie Taylor

THREE RIVERS PRESS • NEW YORK

Published by Three Rivers Press, New York, New York.
Member of the Crown Publishing Group.

Random House, Inc. New York, Toronto, London, Sydney, Auckland

www.randomhouse.com

THREE RIVERS PRESS is a registered trademark and the Three Rivers Press colophon is a trademark of Random House, Inc.

Printed in the United States of America

Design by Elizabeth Van Itallie

Library of Congress Cataloging-in-Publication Data

Taylor, Julie.
    The girls' guide to guys: straight talk on flirting, dating, breaking up, making up, and finding true love / Julie Taylor. — 1st ed.
        (pbk.)
        1. Dating (Social customs). 2. Interpersonal attraction. 3. Teenage boys. 4. Teenage girls. I. Title

HQ801 .T294 2000
646.7'7'0835 — dc21

00–029879

0-609-80505-3
First Edition

In memory of my incredible mom,
Freda Taylor (1946–1999),
who taught me everything I know about guys.
I love you and miss you every day.

table of contents

acknowledgments

o many people helped me in the writing of this book. In no particular order, they are:

My agent: Kip Kotzen, who has been a constant support and spent countless hours making sure this book became a reality.

My editors, past and present: Teryn Johnson, Dina Siciliano, Jessica Schulte, Chuck Adams, Lori Berger, Carol Brietzke, Isabel Burton, Laura Corn, Debbie Duenes, Susan Gifford, Barrie Gillies, Jena Hofsted, Kristen Kemp, Jeannie Kim, Lisa Lombardi, Nina Malkin, Beth Mayall, Megan Fitzmorris McCafferty, Jon Smalls, Sabrina Solin, Christine Summer, Malissa Thompson, and everyone at my teen zines: *Twist, Cosmo Girl, YM, Jump, Teen, React, All About You,* and Bolt.com. And extra-special thanks go to the sweet Stephanie Dolgoff, who gave me my very first assignment.

A deep-felt thanks also goes to my amazing friend and relationship expert, Elizabeth Hurchalla (author of the wonderful book *Getting Over Him*), for her special guidance on the breakup chapters. I love you!

My friends: especially Jenni, Stuart and Chris, Eliz H, Zanni and John, Eliz K, Darcy, Sari, Marcy, Ivy, Jodi, Kristen, Char, Janis, Katrina, and Chris and Sue. I love you guys.

My dad and brother: Jim and Jimmy, both of whom have had a very tough year.

My husband: Jay Brown, the coolest and most supportive guy I know, and the "Browns," Alex, Taylor, Robyn, Leo, and Bill. And my cool cat, Little Guy.

Everyone who was so supportive through my mom's illness and in the writing of this book. Betty, Billie, both Traci's, Aunt Ju, Granny, Penny, Shelly, Dean, Jayne, all my cousins, uncles, extended family . . . I could go on and on. I love you all!

Whoever I forgot here . . . I know there will be at least one! My apologies!

All the wonderful girlies who e-mailed me after reading *Franco American Dreams*. Your letters meant so much to me and inspired me to write this book. Thank you.

welcome to guyville

uys. You love 'em, you hate 'em, you can't live without 'em. You wish they'd all drop dead. Depending on the day (or the hour, or the minute, or the millisecond), your opinion of the Y-chromosome variety could change drastically. Sometimes boys are lovable creatures: leaving you sweet notes in your locker, locking eyes with you in English, smiling in that way that makes your knees turn to jelly. At other times, they're infuriating aliens from the planet Jerkury: not calling when they say they will, blowing you off for other (much less cute) girls, or reciting one too many South Park lines during what was supposed to be a romantic moment. How in the world is a cool girl like you supposed to be able to figure these fellas out?

Well, you've come to the right place. *The Girls' Guide to Guys* is a bible for all things boy-related and will tackle issues that Mom has no clue about and discuss topics your friends might be too embarrassed to bring up. First off, I'll show you how to figure out what type of guy he is—from Joe Cool jock to garage-band grunge. Then I'll hold your well-manicured hand through the highs and lows of a killer crush. And, after I show you how to flirt and conquer your first-date jitters, we'll explore how to decide when it's time to promote him to official boyfriend status. You'll also get the lowdown on stuff like making out and fighting fair. In a long-distance relationship? I'll discuss how to survive one of those, too, before going over the do's and don'ts of cyber-love and summer hook-ups. And if your stud turns into a dud, you'll get the 411 on how to deal when he's being lame, when and if to dump his sorry butt, and how to survive if you happen to be the dumpee, not the dumper. And for those of you who are between guys or currently boycotting them altogether, I'll detail all the perks no one tells you about when you go it alone.

And just when you thought it couldn't get any better, there's a quiz at the end of each chapter for you to take. Once you're done, you'll know the answers to such probing questions as "Is He Second-Date Material?" and "Are You Officially Over Him?" and maybe learn a little bit about yourself in the process. Bonus!

The Girls' Guide to Guys is your guide—written by a girl who has been obsessed with boys since her first kiss in second grade from a cute seven-year-old boy named Edward. I'm not saying I have all the answers—I don't. But after countless sweet boyfriends, loser boyfriends, boys who took my number but never called, boys I was in love with who didn't know my name, boys who loved me but I didn't love back, boys I kissed, boys I kissed but then wished I hadn't, boys I obsessed over, boys I obsessively tried to forget, boys I wish I never met, and boys I will never, ever forget, I know a thing or two about the elusive male species. And I'm going to share every last detail with you.

Why? you ask. Because I think most books on this subject are written by forty-year-olds who have no idea what it's like to be a teenager today. And they tell you what they think you want to hear, trying to be all "hip" and "with-it" by using this supposed slang that is so tired it's not even funny. If you wanted a forty-year-old's opinion, you'd ask your mom, and nothing against your mom, but times have changed drastically since she was a teen. You're dealing with way more than they ever had to. Hello—Columbine? AIDS? And with the Web and Kevin Williamson flicks and the zillion teen mags out there, you're naturally a lot more in-the-know than she was at your age, simply because you're exposed to more.

That said, this is a guide you can turn to when you have a question about anything boy-related and know you will always get a straight answer from a girl who knows what the heck is up. And I promise to never talk down to you or treat your relationships like they're no big deal. Because they do matter—a lot. And so do you.

This is the book I wish I had in my hot little hands when I

was your age. A guide I could've gone to when I couldn't figure out why Patrick, my ninth-grade crush, prank-called my house every Friday night but never asked me out. Or when Simon, the stockboy I was seriously in love with, stood me up for that R.E.M. concert after acting like he was so into me the week before. Or that time I was debating about whether or not to ask Todd, this super-hot senior, to the prom, but never got my nerve up. All life-or-death moments in my life I survived, true, but it would've been a lot simpler if I had an instruction manual like this one to steer me along the bumpy road of love, lust, and heartbreak. May this book make your own boy-filled adventures a little less flawsome and a lot more awesome.

Love, Julie

what type of guy is he?

chapter 1

There are a zillion different guys out there with a gazillion different kinds of personalities. But fortunately for anyone who's trying to gain any kind of insight into the boy brain, most fall into at least one general category. Maybe he's the athletic type—a Gatorade-fueled jock who wouldn't be caught dead in any shoes but Jordans. Or maybe he's the sensitive poet — a bereted brooder who's never spotted without his dog-eared copy of *Catcher in the Rye*. Once you figure out what type of guy he is, it's easier to discern whether or not he's the one for you. That's why this chapter details everything you need to know about the top ten boy categories, from his favorite duds to his favorite dead celeb. But since there are always a few fellas who defy description, the following categories won't cover everybody. But, hey, it's a start.

The Brainiac

He makes straight A's and is the kind of guy who would give Will Hunting a run for his money in the brains department. You want to show him there's more to life than homework. Here's what makes Mr. Genius tick:

- **Favorite duds:** White oxfords, dark-blue jeans, and tennis shoes
- **Dead giveaway:** His three-ring binders stuffed with notes, assignments, and worksheets
- **Favorite drink:** Carrot juice
- **Favorite word:** Valedictorian
- **What he'll be:** Doctor, attorney, rocket scientist
- **After-school jobs:** Lab technician, law-office intern, library aide
- **Never misses:** Anything on PBS
- **Favorite dead celebrity:** Albert Einstein
- **Where he'll take you:** To a lecture
- **Topics to dish with him:** Medical breakthroughs, last week's AP exam, world politics
- **Girl qualities that attract him:** Intelligent, good listener, driven, dedicated
- **Girl qualities that distract him:** Social, carefree, slacker, low SAT scores
- **Choose him if:** He's ambitious, hard-working, and caring

- **Lose him if:** He's condescending, antisocial, or overbearing
- **Word to the wise:** Brainiacs are sometimes so preoccupied by their own high IQ that they lose sight of the fact that there's more to life than getting into Harvard. If you feel like he cares more about his college essay than he cares about you, say "See ya!"
- **The ex files:** "Jack was the smartest guy in the world. I was totally turned on by how much he knew and how much he taught me. While my other boyfriends would take me to the movies, he took me to the symphony. We talked about stuff that mattered—like politics and art. He went to school two thousand miles away, so we grew apart. But I'll always remember him." —Lori, 18

The Best Bud

He's the kind of guy you can tell anything and everything to, someone who makes you feel totally at ease. He treats you like a true-blue friend, but you'd like to be elevated to the position of girlfriend. Here's all you need to know to score the promotion:

- **Favorite duds:** Polos, khakis, and loafers
- **Dead giveaway:** His thousand-watt pearly-white grin
- **Favorite drink:** Homemade lemonade

- **Favorite word:** Buddy
- **What he'll be:** PR exec, advertising whiz, counselor
- **After-school jobs:** Grocery stockboy, video clerk, day-care worker
- **Never misses:** *Friends*
- **Favorite dead celebrity:** Will Rogers
- **Where he'll take you:** To a happening party
- **Topics to dish with him:** Your deepest thoughts and feelings, mutual acquaintances, future plans
- **Girl qualities that attract him:** Open, candid, trustworthy, dependable
- **Girl qualities that distract him:** Unemotional, gossipy, dishonest, erratic
- **Choose him if:** He's sweet, unselfish, and reliable
- **Lose him if:** He's overly mushy, uncommitted, or whipped
- **Word to the wise:** The main problem with the Best Bud is that you might not be the only girl he's letting cry on his shoulder. Often they have more than one "bud" on the line. Make sure you're the only one before spilling your deepest and darkest secrets.
- **The ex files:** "The best kind of boyfriends are ones who are your friends first. Like Jerome. We hung out for a while as friends. He even helped me get over this really bad breakup, and never tried anything at all. After hanging with him for about four months, I came to this revelation

that I liked him as more than just a friend. And we dated for two years after that." —Tyonna, 19

The Anarchist

He's mad as hell at all the world's injustices, and is certain he alone can make a difference. You're turned on by his passion and want to help him fight the good fight. Below, the lowdown on your de facto dude.

- **Favorite duds:** Anything black
- **Dead giveaway:** The Sex Pistols sticker on his locker
- **Favorite drink:** Any liquid he's not old enough to buy yet
- **Favorite word:** Rebellion
- **What he'll be:** ACLU lawyer, independent-film director, Peace Corps volunteer
- **After-school jobs:** PETA volunteer, investigative reporter, record-store clerk
- **Never misses:** Anything on the Independent Film Channel
- **Favorite dead celebrity:** Sid Vicious
- **Where he'll take you:** To a Tibetan Freedom Concert
- **Topics to dish with him:** How much your hometown sucks, how much your teachers suck, how much America sucks
- **Girl qualities that attract him:** Hot-tempered, militant, idealistic, unafraid

- **Girl qualities that distract him:** Worrisome, quiet, cares what others think, fades into the woodwork
- **Choose him if:** He's self-assertive, confident, and passionate
- **Lose him if:** He's dictatorial, violent, or invective
- **Word to the wise:** When the Anarchist uses his hostility to fight against animal testing or ozone depletion, it's cool. But if he directs that hostility toward you, it's not cool.
- **The ex files:** "My ex, Brian, was this real revolutionary guy. He listened to ska and was always boycotting products for one reason or another. All his friends were like that, too. But after a few months of being together, he developed this whole attitude about me eating meat. I was finally like, 'Listen, if you want to be a vegetarian that's fine, but I'm not becoming one just because you want me to.' We broke up soon thereafter." —Jennifer, 16

The Future President

This is the sort of guy who runs for student government because

he really cares what the prom theme is or whether or not you get an extended lunch hour. Aw! He's passionate about changing the world, and you're certain he could change your world for the better. Here, everything you need to know about your political prince.

- **Favorite duds:** Anything from Banana Republic, Abercrombie and Fitch, or J. Crew; preferably dry-clean only
- **Dead giveaway:** Super-short hair that's even more styled than yours
- **Favorite drink:** Orange juice for extra Vitamin C
- **Favorite word:** Resumé
- **What he'll be:** Politician, CEO, stockbroker
- **After-school jobs:** Bank teller, Gap salesman, local newspaper reporter
- **Never misses:** *Politically Incorrect*
- **Favorite dead celebrity:** JFK Jr.
- **Where he'll take you:** A pizza party at the campaign headquarters he volunteers at
- **Topics to dish with him:** The latest D.C. scandal, world events, front-page news
- **Girl qualities that attract him:** Patriotism, go-getter attitude, classic good looks, intellect
- **Girl qualities that distract him:** MTV addiction, anti-establishment world-view, apathy, cluelessness
- **Choose him if:** He's smart, super-involved, and actually *cares* about something
- **Lose him if:** He's cocky, self-involved, or needs everyone to love him
- **Word to the wise:** The major glitch with a future-president-type is that he's so busy, he might not always have time

for you. And since they're so skilled in telling people what they want to hear, you might not always be able to believe every single word he says.

- **The ex files:** "I dated our class vice president. He was all uptight and driven and single-minded. After awhile, I felt like I was just someone he was happy to be seen with but not exactly an appreciated girlfriend. Eventually I got sick of it and broke it off. I hear he went to college in D.C. If he ever runs for president, I won't vote for him." —Summer, 21

The Class Clown

He's so hilarious, he puts Tom Green to shame. You're sure you'd be his perfect sidekick: Lucy to his Ricky, Dharma to his Greg. Read on for the facts on your foxy funnyman.

- **Favorite duds:** South Park T's, cargo pants, and beat-up Chuck Taylors
- **Dead giveaway:** That loud, booming voice (which ensures everyone will hear his one-liners)
- **Favorite drink:** Yoo-Hoo
- **Favorite word:** Farting
- **What he'll be:** Comedian, game-show host, actor
- **After-school jobs:** Toy-store clerk, team mascot, one of those survey guys at the mall

- **Never misses:** *King of the Hill*
- **Favorite dead celebrity:** Chris Farley
- **Where he'll take you:** To an Adam Sandler film fest
- **Topics to dish with him:** Who's funnier, Chris Rock or Chris Tucker, the weekly lineup of Comedy Central, how hilarious his latest prank was
- **Girl qualities that attract him:** Humorous, wild, uninhibited, not easily embarrassed
- **Girl qualities that distract him:** Studious, quiet, shy, reserved
- **Choose him if:** He's fun, clever, and entertaining
- **Lose him if:** He's lewd, crude, or cracks jokes at your expense
- **Word to the wise:** The Class Clown can bring loads of laughs into your life. But if he can never get serious—especially during romantic moments—the joke may be on him.
- **The ex files:** "The sweetest guy I ever dated was a Class Clown type. He cracked me up, and we had the greatest time together. But the best thing was that underneath his joke-a-minute exterior, he could be really sweet. He used to leave the funniest answering machine messages. He moved away, so we had to break up. But he still holds a special place in my heart." —Francine, 16

The Musician

He taps out rockin' riffs on his math book and scribbles song lyrics in the margins of his Bio notes. And when you hear Limp Biskit tunes blaring from his car as he squeals his way into the parking lot, your heart literally skips a beat. He's so sensitive and artistic, you're convinced the two of you could make beautiful music together. Read on for the skinny on your soul stud.

- **Favorite duds:** Anything black, flannel, or secondhand, bonus points if it's leather
- **Dead giveaway:** The band bumper stickers all over his beat-up car
- **Favorite drink:** Anything dispensed from a keg
- **Favorite word:** Dude
- **What he'll be:** Rock star, producer, music critic
- **After-school jobs:** Record-store clerk, stereo salesman, bar mitzvah singer
- **Never misses:** *Biorhythm*
- **Favorite dead celebrity:** Kurt Cobain
- **Where he'll take you:** To hear his band practice
- **Topics to dish with him:** The latest Kid Rock single, the suckiness of Top 40 music, how much he rocks
- **Girl qualities that attract him:** An expansive CD collection, funky fashion sense, musical, high "cool" quotient

- **Girl qualities that distract him:** Hypercritical opinions, uptight attitude, super preppy style, starving for attention
- **Choose him if:** He's creative, sensitive, and a great listener
- **Lose him if:** He's stuck-up, oblivious to your problems, or blows you off for his bandmates
- **Word to the wise:** The biggest potential problem when hooking up with the Musician is his tendency to put his music first and everything else second. And if you're used to getting a lot of attention, taking a backseat to his bass will really blow.
- **The ex files:** "George Governor. That was the stage name of my drum-banging boyfriend. I spent a lot of time going to his gigs. It was kind of exciting, like I was dating Eddie Vedder or something. We eventually grew apart, but I still listen to his CD sometimes. I consider my time with him my groupie experience and wouldn't trade it for the world." —June, 19

The Poet

He writes sonnets during Spanish and haikus during Home Ec. He's so deep and mysterious, you're dying to find out all there is to know about this elusive artist. Here are a few insights on your Shakespeare in Love.

- **Favorite duds:** Cords, stocking caps, and thrift-store suit jackets
- **Dead giveaway:** That black journal he's always scribbling in
- **Favorite drink:** Espresso
- **Favorite word:** Esoteric
- **What he'll be:** Writer, college professor, coffee shop owner
- **After-school jobs:** Bookstore clerk, library assistant, Starbucks coffee jockey
- **Never misses:** A&E's *Biography*
- **Favorite dead celebrity:** Jack Kerouac
- **Where he'll take you:** To a planetarium
- **Topics to dish with him:** Hemingway's alcoholism, how much John Grisham (or any other best-selling author) sucks, *The New Yorker*
- **Girl qualities that attract him:** Extremely well-read, sarcastic, independent, bohemian-cool
- **Girl qualities that distract him:** Cliquish, shallow, giggly, slave to the TV
- **Choose him if:** He's introspective, thoughtful, and talented
- **Lose him if:** He's moody, tortured, or pretentious
- **Word to the wise:** Poets who are too busy being "deep" to have a good time can be a major drag. And if all he talks about is how much life sucks, it's easy to start believing the hype.
- **The ex files:** "I got the sweetest poems in the world from

my poet boyfriend. I still have every one of them in this shoe box. I look at them sometimes. There's something so sweet about a boy who will actually put pen to paper for you. It's like old-fashioned or something." —April, 16

The Jock

He's so talented and in shape, you could easily see him gracing the cover of *Sports Illustrated* someday. And you'd like nothing better than to be his number-one girl cheering him on from the sidelines. How do you catch this mile-a-minute muscleman? Take notes.

- **Favorite duds:** Tank tops, sweats, and designer sneakers
- **Dead giveaway:** Those huge muscles bulging out of his shirtsleeves
- **Favorite drink:** Powerade
- **Favorite words:** "Take State!"
- **What he'll be:** Coach, professional athlete, gym owner
- **After-school jobs:** Lawn mower, personal trainer, Little League Ref
- **Never misses:** ESPN's *SportsCenter*
- **Favorite dead celebrity:** Babe Ruth
- **Where he'll take you:** To Friday night's game

- **Topics to dish with him:** Steroids and their effect on the libido, how he played last week, who'll win the Super Bowl
- **Girl qualities that attract him:** Enthusiastic, school spirit, supportive, loyal
- **Girl qualities that distract him:** Disinterest in sports, self-absorbed, alternative, cynical
- **Choose him if:** He's driven, super-athletic, and full of life
- **Lose him if:** He's single-minded, egotistical, or mean
- **Word to the wise:** Since the Jock is used to being a celeb on the field, he might expect the same red-carpet treatment in a relationship. And being a supporting player to his starring role can get old quick.
- **The ex files:** "Senior year, I dated the quarterback of the football team. He was actually a total jerk who rambled on and on about what plays he made and how bad-ass he was. I told him he needed to face reality: He wasn't Troy Aikman and never would be. We parted on very ugly terms, but it felt good to knock him down a few pegs." —Rosie, 18

The Cyberjunkie

He's a super-smart sweetie who's got his finger on the pulse of the on-line revolution. You know his e-mail address, sure, but the rest of him remains a mystery. Until now . . .

- **Favorite duds:** Rumpled T-shirts, ragged Levi's, eighties digital watch
- **Dead giveaway:** His yellowish pallor—the result of too much computer time and not enough sun
- **Favorite drink:** Anything with ginkgo
- **Favorite word:** Dot-com
- **What he'll be:** Computer programmer, Web designer, Silicon Valley mogul
- **After-school jobs:** Computer lab technician, chat-room host, arcade employee
- **Never misses:** *The X-Files*
- **Favorite dead celebrity:** J. Presper Eckert (co-inventor of the world's first digital computer)
- **Where he'll take you:** To a comic book convention
- **Topics to dish with him:** Modem speeds, the stock price of Yahoo, AOL vs. independent Internet providers
- **Girl qualities that attract him:** Articulate, Web-savvy, idealistic, goal-driven
- **Girl qualities that distract him:** Fear of technology, fashion-obsessed, social butterfly, extrovert
- **Choose him if:** He's inventive, intelligent, and visionary
- **Lose him if:** He's alienated, sullen, or chained to his computer twenty-four hours-a-day
- **Word to the wise:** Cyberjunkies spend so much time on-line that many have no clue how to live in the real world. If

he'd rather e-mail you than see you in person, it's time to sign off.

- **The ex files:** "I got the best e-mails from Jeremy. We actually met on-line, in this teen chatroom. I remember when I'd see I had mail from him, my heart would start beating really fast. After we e-mailed for a few months, we agreed to go on a double date since he lived in the next town over. But when we met face-to-face, he wasn't my type. We clicked on paper but not in person. But I still hear from him sometimes." —Robin, 15

The Partier

He's a starry-eyed dreamer who likes to party and have a good time. You're the sort of Alanis-style spiritualist who could light up his life. Here, some hippie homework . . .

- **Favorite duds:** Jean jackets, concert T's, and leather moccasin boots
- **Dead giveaway:** The fact that he's always hanging in the backseat of his smoke-filled car
- **Favorite drink:** 40s of malt liquor
- **Favorite word:** Killer
- **What he'll be:** Roadie, concert promoter, *High Times* reporter

- **After-school jobs:** Record-store clerk, vo-tech student, professional skateboarder
- **Never misses:** *Beavis and Butthead* reruns
- **Favorite dead celebrity:** Jerry Garcia
- **Where he'll take you:** To an outdoor concert
- **Topics to dish with him:** Rainbow gatherings, where the happening party is, his favorite Phish song
- **Girl qualities that attract him:** Mellow, laid-back, experimental, hippie-fied
- **Girl qualities that distract him:** Trendy, uptight, afraid to try new things, homebody
- **Choose him if:** He's open-minded, philosophical, and unselfish
- **Lose him if:** He's abusive, in his own world, or utterly wasted.
- **Word to the wise:** Not every Partier is into illegal substances, but he did get that pesky nickname somehow. If he's abusing drugs, he's not worth your time, bottom line.
- **The ex-files:** "I once dated a guy who was constantly bent over his bong. The more attention he paid to his weed, the less attention he paid to me. And since we were never in the same place emotionally, how could we be in a relationship? I finally dumped him for someone who appreciated me in a way he never could." —Gillian, 17

who's your dream date?

1. Before your dream date, your ideal man would bring you:

a) a rhyme he wrote especially for you.

b) a bouquet of daisies.

c) Pez.

d) a framed copy of the first e-mail you ever sent him.

e) a sixer of wine coolers.

2. You and your man decide to rent a video. You suggest:

a) an edgy independent film.

b) an action-packed blockbuster.

c) a romantic comedy.

d) a slapstick, rolling-in-the-aisles satire.

e) a psychological thriller.

3. In your spare time, you like to:

a) surf the Internet.

b) go to games and rallys.

c) listen to music or read.

d) hit the cool, underground spots.

e) hang with your buds.

4. Who would you most want to be your boyfriend?

a) Someone you can always rely on

b) Someone who's super-social and involved

c) Someone who's very adventurous

d) Someone who's artistic and expressive

e) Someone who's intelligent and thoughtful

5. Of the following, which TV character is most your type?

    a) Angel from *Angel*

    b) Noel from *Felicity*

    c) Dawson from *Dawson's Creek*

    d) Tommy from *3rd Rock*

    e) Eli from *Once and Again*

6. It's your birthday. Your dream date would:

    a) dedicate a song to you on the radio.

    b) score a touchdown in your honor.

    c) throw you a surprise birthday celebration.

    d) take you to a rockin' all-ages dance club.

    e) plaster his website with pictures of you.

7. Which celeb's style do you most embody?

    a) Neve Campbell

    b) Monica

    c) Rose McGowan

    d) Keri Russell

    e) Gabrielle Reese

8. What's your favorite kind of music?

    a) Rap

    b) Alternative

    c) Hard Rock

    d) Techno

    e) Top 40

9. What's your favorite date outfit?

a) Jeans and a T
b) Your trendiest threads
c) Khakis and tailored shirt
d) Anything tight and form-fitting
e) Flowing sarong and peasant blouse

10. You're going out to eat on a first date. Where do you suggest?

a) A hole-in-the-wall Mexican joint
b) The place in the mall where everybody goes
c) That hilariously cheesy theme restaurant
d) A quiet diner
e) A cool coffee shop

Scoring:

1. a) 1; b) 3; c) 4; d) 5; e) 2   **6.** a) 1; b) 4; c) 3; d) 2; e) 5
2. a) 1; b) 2; c) 3; d) 4; e) 5   **7.** a) 3; b) 1; c) 2; d) 5; e) 4
3. a) 5; b) 4; c) 1; d) 2; e) 3   **8.** a) 4; b) 1; c) 2; d) 5; e) 3
4. a) 3; b) 4; c) 2; d) 1; e) 5   **9.** a) 5; b) 4; c) 3; d) 2; e) 1
5. a) 2; b) 5; c) 1; d) 4; e) 3   **10.** a) 2; b) 3; c) 4; d) 5; e) 1

Now add up your score to discover your dream date.

10–18: The Tortured Soul

Boys who are creative and artistic totally mash your potatoes.
You adore the poems he scrawls on napkins and the ballads he
rattles off to you on your way to school. Sweet! Being his
muse—and his biggest fan—rocks your world, but you never

consider yourself a groupie. That's because you're his equal—
not just a hanger-on. Go, girl! When it comes to dating, skip
dinner and a movie—you need culture, excitement, and glam-
our. Taking you to art museums, concerts, and book signings are
the easiest ways to win you over. And since you're in love with
being in love, never fear—The Tortured Soul will provide you
with loads of romance, drama, and adventure.

Love Connections: The Poet, the Musician

19–27: Rebel Without a Cause

A guy who oozes danger and excitement really revs your engine.
You love the way he's always at the hottest parties or right in the
middle of the latest school scandal. You're into hanging with
this black sheep because you're one of the few people who
actually understands him. He's so deep, intriguing, and mysterious, he makes all the other guys you know look like Boy Scouts!
When you're out with him, you're not just on a date—you're on
an adventure, something you can tell your grandkids about
someday. Whether you're protesting the mistreatment of the rain
forests or simply partying like it's 2099, there's never a dull
moment when you're with the Rebel Without a Cause. As long
as you don't break any laws in the process, have fun making history with this wild-eyed wanderer.

Love Connections: The Anarchist, the Partier

28–35: America's Most Wanted

Forget flowers, romance, and all that mushy stuff—you just want a guy you can depend on. You're totally into the way he can magically cheer you up, no matter how down you're feeling. And since you like your boyfriend to also be your friend, this is a perfect match. You can tell him anything and everything—and you know that your secrets are always safe. And he'll always remember important anniversaries—like your first date and the day you officially became boyfriend-girlfriend. Since he's so popular and well connected, you'll always be invited to the coolest gatherings—a definite bonus for super-social you. Hold on to this keeper!

Love Connections: The Best Bud, the Future President

35–42: Show-Off Stud

You're a sucker for a guy in the spotlight. His confidence, charisma, and charm melt your heart like margarine in a microwave. Being his girlfriend means you enjoy your share of the glare, too, and that's fine by you, because you're ready for

 your close-up. When you two go out on the town, you gravitate toward places you can see and be seen—like local celebrities, you make the rounds of all the most happening parties and places. And since you both love talking to others and

being in the heart of the action, you're a scorching couple both in and out of the limelight.

Love Connections: The Jock, the Class Clown

43–50: Señor Smarty Pants

Boys with astronomical IQs raise your interest. You love the way he'll stay up with you all night to help you cram for your English exam and the fact that he sends you the cutest e-mails on earth. Being with someone you can have an actual conversation with about what's going on in the Middle East and things that actually matter is so refreshing. He celebrates your intelligence rather than being intimidated by it, which is a major point in his favor. And the fact that he doesn't have a slacker bone in his body doesn't hurt, either. When you go out, he'll actually take you to a symphony without kicking and screaming like most other guys would. Latch on to this brilliant boy wonder!

Love Connections: The Brainiac, the Cyberjunkie

majorly crushed

You're in love with him. For real. You think about him day and night. You doodle his name all over your notebooks. You pair your first name with his last name just for effect. And you haven't even had a date with the guy! You, my friend, are in the throes of a killer crush, and they don't call them "crushes" for nothing. The emotions they deliver can crush you like a gigantic wave, leaving you utterly dumbfounded. Suddenly, in his presence, you can't eat, walk, even form a sentence. It's like he's the drug and you're the junkie—addicted.

Crushes are totally normal. I personally have had hundreds of crushes in my lifetime, ranging in intensity from oh-that-guy's-cute to I-love-him-I-love-him-I-love-him. Crushing hard on a guy is so fun. Instantly, your life is filled with drama and intrigue.

I-WANT-HIM ENTERTAINMENT

Want to do something about your crush without letting him know you like him straight out? Go for it . . . .

♥ Keep a notebook to chronicle your feelings about him. You'll have a blast reading it down the road.

♥ See how many words you can spell from the letters in his name.

♥ Write him a letter telling him exactly how you feel about him, but don't send it.

♥ Send him a Valentine from his secret admirer just for kicks.

♥ Wink at him from across a crowded room. If he calls you on it, you can always claim you had something on your contact!

When will you see him next? Should you say anything? What will you wear? Once I had a crush on a Bennigan's waiter and I wore a different outfit every single time I went into the restaurant (which was two or three times a week). I'd leave him notes with his tips and on his car. I was totally off the deep end! But the thing about crushes is: They're safe. You experience that jolt that comes from liking someone without going through the actual highs and lows of a relationship. You can fantasize about how good you guys would be together—and the reality will never disrupt the fantasy.

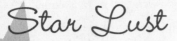

Star Lust

A gorgeous celebrity is a prime crush target. You pin his pictures on your wall and have seen every one of his movies at least ten times. If he's a singer, you know every one of his songs by heart and constantly have his CD on repeat-play. You're certain that if he met you, you'd be together forever.

Everybody has a crush on a celeb at least once in her lifetime. These stars seem so much larger-than-life: glamorous, rich, totally hot. And they're always in your face—in record stores or movie theaters, on TV or magazine covers. It's like you can't escape them. And what guy in your school is cuter than Leonardo DiCaprio? Probably nobody. Which makes your crush even stronger.

Plus, a celeb is about the safest crush you can have. The odds of you ever actually coming face-to-face with him are slim-to-none, but you can still have the thrill of being into a guy. You can buy unauthorized biographies on him and memorize stuff like his birthday and favorite food. And you can write him fan letters without fear of him showing them around school or ridiculing you for it. It's like you get to love a boy without that possibility-of-rejection thing screwing things up. Yea!

And crushing on a star can be good practice for the real thing. You can get used to those flutters in your stomach when you see him. And get familiar with what it feels like to think about a guy like all the time. And when you finally meet a "real" guy who makes you feel this way, you won't be so freaked out or confused. Because you've already felt this way before and lived to tell the tale.

But I don't want to dash all your dreams here. If you're utterly convinced that you're going to end up marrying a Backstreet Boy and don't want to hear otherwise, there is a glimmer of hope. *Beverly Hills 90210* veteran Luke Perry (you know, the one who looks like he's forty) married one of his fans, whom he met after she mailed him a letter. So, even though the chances are maybe a million to one, it does happen now and again. So keep dreaming. Because sometimes dreams do come true.

Crushes on Friends

Another big crush target: the guy friend. They creep up on you, too—like something out of *The Blair Witch Project*. You've never liked him like that before and then—boom, you don't know what hit you. It's as if before this moment you've had blinders on, and now you can see for the first time just how perfect he really is. The tricky thing about having a crush on a friend is that you could jeopardize the friendship by coming clean with your feelings. If he doesn't like you in the same way, it could get a little awkward. Suddenly the friendship isn't the same. So you've not only lost your crush, you've lost a good friend.

The upside of this, of course, is that if he does like you back, it could be the beginning of an awesome relationship.

You're already friends, so you're comfortable around each other. You obviously enjoy each other's company. Major long-term potential, no doubt about it.

What should you do? I suggest following the one-month rule here. If you're really crushing on him hard for at least a month, you should then proceed with caution. Before this window period has expired, it's too risky to tell him how you feel since it could just be a passing fancy. Why jeopardize the friendship if you won't even like him that way next week? But once you're sure that you really do like him, you owe it to yourself to tell him. Because you could be missing out on the best thing ever if you don't take a chance.

Crushes on (Way) Older Guys

The cute science teacher, your friend's older brother, your next-

door neighbor—who hasn't had a crush on an older, sophisticated guy? Dating (or crushing on) someone a little older is no big deal, but if you're after someone who's old enough to be your dad, that's another story. As long as it never goes beyond the "crush" stage, however, it's harmless. Because of his

advanced age, the guy is totally unattainable anyway. Having a crush on an older guy is like a mini-version of having one on a celeb—it's safe and fun. The only way you could get into trouble here is if you really start pursuing, say, a teacher. It's bad news and could get you thrown out of school or charged with sexual harassment. Enough said!

If a way-older man is pursuing you, that's even more danger-ous—it's against the law, for one thing (if you're under eighteen), and he's completely taking advantage of you. Even if a teacher says he's in love with you or something, it's still abuse. So if you're being harassed by a teacher or an adult, tell someone you trust, like a counselor or family member. They can help.

Are You Crushing Too Hard?

Whether you're into a celebrity or a real-life guy, a harmless crush can sometimes elevate to harmful proportions. That's because there's a very thin line between admiration and obses-sion. Remember Alicia Silverstone in *The Crush*? Here, some signs that you're entering *Fatal Attraction* land:

- **You think about him literally twenty-four hours a day. You can't study, eat, or sleep because of these thoughts.**
- **You drive by his house or work more than six times a day.**
- **You call his house and prank-call him more than three times a day.**

- You're turning down date offers because you don't want to betray your crush.
- You have fantasies about getting rid of his girlfriend so you can be together.
- You take pictures of him from afar with a telephoto lens.
- You follow him around like a spy just to see where he's going.

If you're guilty of any of the above, you need to talk to somebody about your feelings. Seek out a school counselor or trusted friend and let them know what's going on. Your behavior is becoming stalkerlike, and in some states you could even be arrested for it.

Kicking It Up a Notch

Many healthy crushes can be the beginning of something really cool—if you take it to the next level, that is. But doing so involves some major risk. What if your crush doesn't like you in the same way you like him? Or what if he's not the guy you thought he was? Are you willing to trade in your dreams for reality? Plus, there's the question of whether or not to make the first move. Should you just confess your feelings? Flirt outrageously? Have a friend spill the beans?

Before you take things a step further, think it over carefully. Are you crushing on this guy just because you want to have

CRUSHING ON A GIRL

Everyone fanta-
sizes about
the same sex
every now and
again—it's totally nor-
mal. But if you find that
your fantasies almost exclu-
sively feature the female sex,
you might be bi or gay. Which
is totally okay! Some of my best
friends are gay. But since this isn't
The Girls' Guide to Girls, I can't give
this subject the attention it deserves
here. Contact the National Gay and Lesbian Hotline
at 1-888-843-4564 for more info. You're not alone.

a crush on someone, or because you really like him? If you're bowled over by his good looks, does he have a personality to match? Is he really someone you'd want to be in a relationship with?

If the answer is yes and you do decide to fess up to him, a safe way to gauge his feelings is to ask him out to a "friends" thing first. Tell him a group of pals are going somewhere and ask if he wants to tag along. This way, if he says no, it's not exactly a personal rejection. Plus, he doesn't get that ego boost from knowing how much you like him. But if he does say yes, you have the buffer of the group date to feel out the vibes.

Writing him a letter confessing your feelings is tempting but could be overkill, especially if he doesn't like you that way. You never want to put something in writing, because you don't know what he's going to do with the note. In a perfect world, he'd hang it on his wall and keep it forever. But if he's a jerk, he could show it to other people or post it on his Web site. Don't take the chance until you know him a little better.

Moving On

Most crushes fizzle out before anything major happens. You meet someone else you like. He does something to make you mad. Or you just get tired of thinking about him. All of this is totally normal behavior. Crushes are like little bridges that get you from one place to the next. Maybe you need to have a crush right now rather than endure the pressure of a serious relationship. Or maybe crushing on this guy will teach you something about yourself that will make you a more enlightened person. Who knows. The important thing is to have fun with it—because crushes can be totally entertaining! The next time you find yourself falling in lust with a guy and know you're on the brink of a colossal crush, go with it. It's like a roller-coaster ride. You'll feel tons of excitement, have a great time, and it will be over before you know it. Just fasten your seat belt and enjoy the ride.

how major is your crush?

1. When you spot your crush in the halls, what do you do?

    a) Smile at him and make eye contact

    b) Keep on trucking

    c) Freeze in place, because you can't even deal

2. You're going to a party and you know your crush is going to be there. How long do you spend getting ready?

    a) More than forty minutes

    b) Twenty to forty minutes

    c) Less than twenty minutes

3. You're watching your *Titanic* video (again). When you see Jack kissing Rose, you:

    a) think it's sweet, but don't specifically think about your crush.

    b) wish it was you and your crush smooching instead.

    c) sigh, then wish you had a boyfriend like that.

4. Your crush's b-day is coming up. You:

    a) send him a card anonymously.

    b) treat it like any other day.

    c) try to find out what he's doing that night.

5. A girl in your English class mentions she hung out with your crush last weekend. You:

      a) are so filled with jealousy, you want to scream.

      b) pump her for details.

      c) figure she's dating him now and move on.

6. You see your crush at the movies buying tickets for a flick you've already seen—and hated. You:

      a) do nothing.

      b) see it again anyway, just so you can be in the same theater.

      c) warn him that it sucks.

7. Your crush is having a big bash and you're not invited. You:

      a) try your hardest to score an invite.

      b) drive by his house while the party is in full swing to watch the action.

      c) blow it off.

8. Your best friend is having a sleepover the same night your crush will be at the game. You:

      a) bail on the party so you can sit in the stands.

      b) kind of wish you could see your crush, but go to the party anyway.

      c) go to the party without a second thought.

Scoring:

1. a) 2; b) 3; c) 1	**5.** a) 1; b) 2; c) 3
2. a) 1; b) 2; c) 3	**6.** a) 3; b) 1; c) 2
3. a) 3; b) 1; c) 2	**7.** a) 2; b) 1; c) 3
4. a) 1; b) 3; c) 2	**8.** a) 1; b) 2; c) 3

Now tally up you score to find out if your crush is colossal or inconsequential!

8–13: Majorly Major

If you took a test on your crush right this very second, you would definitely score 110 percent, hands down. You have this boy on the brain so big-time, it's a wonder there's room for anything else. While it is totally fine to be into someone, blowing off all your friends and responsibilities because you're thinking about him all day, every day is very unhealthy. Not only will your relationships and grades suffer, it's easy to lose sight of what's important when you set all your sights on your crush. Instead of making him number one in your life, make yourself number one. Your crush will be way healthier, and you'll be much happier in the long run.

14–19: Moderately Major

You do think about your crush a bit much sometimes, but you also keep your feelings in check by valuing all the other stuff in your life. You're very much into your friends, family, school, and extracurriculars—and would never drop all of that over a crush, no matter how cute he was. Although, truth be told, you have been guilty of occasionally obsessing over Mr. Right (and who hasn't?), you know you have too much of a life to solely devote it to a guy. Period.

20–24: Next to Nonexistent

You don't feel your crush deserves any more attention than, say, what you're having for dinner or even tomorrow's math assignment. Although it's fine not to focus solely on boys, the reason you tend to diminish your on-fire feelings may just be because you're freaked about liking someone in that way. After all, having a crush means you're acknowledging your feelings and allowing yourself to explore them—pretty scary stuff! While you don't have to go completely bonkers over your crush, feeling excited when he says "hi" or thinking about him on your way to lunch doesn't mean you're out of control—it simply means you're a girl with a crush. And that can be a pretty fun thing to be.

flirt alert

ou see a cute guy. You smile. Make eye contact. Flip your hair over your shoulder. Laugh your cutest laugh. Do whatever you have to do to get his attention. It's called flirting, and every girl does it—even if she doesn't know she's doing it. But what are the best ways to go about it? My best friend in college seemed to have a secret power over guys, and I wanted to know how to get it. I asked her one day how she got so good at flirting—and she told me it came naturally to her, like breathing. If you're one of these guy-magnet girls, I commend you. But for those who need a little more direction (like I did), this chapter is full of techniques, pointers, and little-known facts guaranteed to fuel your flirting forces.

Location, Location, Location

Before you can actually flirt with gorgeous guys, you have to know where to find them. Sure, there's the obvious answer, school — yet if yours is anything like mine was, there's probably a major shortage of cuties there. But don't stress. There are plenty of other places to meet cool guys. Here are my five favorites.

1. The Mall

This is a prime place to meet boys because you've got the customers and the employees to choose from! And there are always guys milling about the food court just waiting for you to make your move. Happy hunting!

2. Your After—School Job

You're in it for the paycheck, I know, but a major perk to minimum-wage monotony is the man-meeting possibilities. Restaurants, video stores, and record stores are especially overrun with the male persuasion. Clock me in!

3. The Pool or Beach

This one is only applicable during the summertime, but when the heat is on, the boys are out in full force. Slip on your favorite swimsuit and gear up for some major fun in the sun!

4. The Movies

You can't meet boys while the movie is going on, obviously, but before and after the flick, the lobby is crawling with cuties. In fact, watching the guys hanging about beforehand is even more fun than watching the coming attractions! Enjoy the show.

5. The Park

They're everywhere—walking their dogs, riding their bikes, playing touch football. And you're right there in the heart of it—jogging, Rollerblading, doing your thing. It's inevitable that you'll meet a cute guy or two at the park without even trying. Ah, the great outdoors!

The Final Four

Since you've never had flirting lessons, how are you supposed to decide which moves are swell and which ones are from hell? Here are four tactics that are guaranteed to make him sit up and take notice.

1. Strut Your Stuff

You find yourself talking a little louder when he's within earshot, and casually drop each and every one of your accomplishments into the conversation. Your motto? If you've got it, flaunt it!

- FLIRT PERK: You'll get his attention immediately while

earning instant recognition. Your guy—and everyone else in the room—can't help but notice you're a shining star!

• FLIRT ALERT: Since every guy in the room will hear how great you are, you might have to fight off the fellows with a stick. But talking too loud could send some scrambling for earplugs . . . or lead them to believe you're stuck-up.

2. Friends First

The guy you like is so lovable, he obviously has friends. So you chat up his pals in the hopes that they'll offer some insight into your man or suggest a group outing or something.

• FLIRT PERK: Since you're not wild over his pals, you'll feel much less nervous than you would talking to him. And this way they can always tell your crush what a sweetheart you are.

• FLIRT ALERT: A too-friendly approach could make the object of your affection think you like his one of his pals, which would instantly render you off-limits!

3. Rescue 911

You spot a hot guy at a party. When you decide he's dateworthy, you go up and "accidentally" drop something like an earring or your purse, then let him help you pick it up. Then, before he knows what hit him, you pick him up.

• FLIRT PERK: This makes him feel good because he thinks he's doing you a favor. And it's a perfect conversation-starter.

• FLIRT ALERT: If you spill a drink all over yourself for

attention, you might get a wrecked outfit out of the deal—and little else!

4. Indirect Communication

You spot one of his buds at the baseball game. You go up to him and "just happen" to mention you think his friend is cute . . . *really* cute!

- FLIRT PERK: Since most people can't keep a secret, your compliment is almost guaranteed to reach the ears of your *amore*. And there's not a guy alive who doesn't like to hear that someone thinks he's cute.

- FLIRT ALERT: There's a lot of guesswork in this one, since you won't know exactly how or when the friend will spill the beans. And the waiting game is enough to drive anyone bonkers!

Top Ten Pickup Lines

Okay, pickup lines are a little cheesy, but sometimes you've got to prepare something to say—or you won't say anything at all. Just for fun, memorize at least one of these lines and promise yourself you'll try it out in the next two weeks. After all, what do you have to lose?

1. "Hey, do you have the notes from Monday?"
By borrowing his notes, you're interacting with him—without being obvious about the fact that you like him. And you're sort

of paying him a compliment by letting him know you trust his note-taking abilities. Plus, you're giving yourself the perfect opportunity to "repay" him by taking him out for cappuccino or a Slurpee. Such a crafty little one, you are.

2. "Have you seen my friend?"

This is a good one to pull when you're at a club or concert. You see a cute guy. You point him out to your friend and instruct her to do a lap around the place. You then approach the guy and tell him you're lost and were wondering if he'd seen your friend. Describe her to him in detail. Being the nice guy he is, he'll probably help you look around for her, and by the time she "happens" to pass by, you'll already know his name and maybe even his phone number.

3. "I like your _____ (shoes, shirt, goatee—fill in the blank)."

Complimenting him on something is the perfect ice-breaker. One time I went up to a guy and told him I liked his Adidas. This ended up segueing into a conversation about how we both liked the Beastie Boys, who are also Adidas fans. From there we ended up talking all night. If you compliment him and mean it, he'll be flattered—and is guaranteed to notice you. Who knows what could happen from there?

4. "What do you want to know about me?"

This is a good one to try if you're feeling particularly gutsy. It will take him by surprise, so you never know what kind of answer you'll get.

5. "I'm having a party on Friday. Wanna come?"

My friend Eliz swears by this one. Every time she throws a bash, she invites every single cute guy she encounters, even if they've barely been introduced. Her parties are always a blast—and very boy-filled—as a result of her bravado.

6. "Have you seen *Scream 14*?"

Asking his opinion about something—like what movie to see on Friday night—is a great conversation-starter. You're showing him you value his opinion and giving him a chance to express himself. And just think about how easily this will lead into: "Want to go see it with me?"

7. "You're the cutest boy here!"

This is a fun one—but it definitely takes guts. I've used it when I felt I was the cutest girl in the room; naturally I should be talking to the cutest boy in the room. He'll be flattered, and his ego will get one heck of a boost. Good lead-in to: "Want to dance?"

8. "What's your story?"

This question is so general, who knows what kind of response you'll get? But that's what's so fun about it.

9. "How do you know so-and-so?"

This is an easy line to use when you're at a party. Obviously you both know the host or you wouldn't be there. So asking him how he knows the Hostess with the Mostest leads to you telling him how you know her and yada yada yada . . . you're off and running.

10. "Isn't this class / assembly / place lame?"

Mutual distaste for something is a great ice-breaker. Sure, it's kind of negative, but you'll instantly have something to talk about. And since you could go on all night about how much the caf's Salisbury steak sucks, you'll get to showcase how articulate and zealous you really are.

Proceed with Caution

Even though flirting can be fun and empowering, there are a few people you should avoid batting your lashes at. An authority figure—like a boss or counselor—is bad news because obviously

you can't date that person, and your flirting could be taken the wrong way. Best to leave that one alone. Ditto for your best friend's boyfriend—because what good could come from that? Even if your flirting is completely harmless, it will probably make her mad and jeopardize your friendship. It's not worth it.

And flirting with someone who's really drunk or on drugs isn't smart either, because you could easily get yourself into a volatile situation you can't handle.

The Ethics of Flirting

If you have a boyfriend, flirting can be a little tricky. Some guys might like it when you flirt with other people, because it reinforces the fact that you're a hot commodity whom other guys are after. Less secure fellows might freak out about it worrying that you're going to dump them or cheat on them. It depends on the guy.

So is it okay to flirt with others when you're attached? It's a question only you can answer. If you're naturally flirty, you shouldn't have to undergo a personality makeover when you're in a relationship. But you also shouldn't go out of your way to make your man feel jealous or insecure.

Employ the "do unto others" rule here. If you'd be upset if he flirted with another girl in front of you, then don't flirt with other guys in front of him. If you do find yourself flirting with someone and your guy goes ballistic, then talk it over with him and set up some guidelines, though that may not always work. When I was dating this guy Paul, I ran into a guy I knew at a bar. We talked for a second, then I walked straight back to where Paul was sitting. He totally lost it! He accused me of cheating on him with the guy I was talking to—even though I had only said hi, and barely knew him. I was infuriated! We talked it out, but broke up a few weeks later when he accused me of kissing somebody else. He obviously had some major insecurities—too big for me to handle. If your guy is irrational about your so-called flirting, maybe he's not the one for you. You have to be the judge.

Top Ten Guy Flirting Moves

1. Punching you in the arm.

Why do guys think punching or poking you is going to make you like them more? Must be something left over from playground days. But if he touches you in any way, it's a major sign of interest.

2. Asking your friend if you're single.

If a guy asks about your dating status, he's interested. This is a safe way for him to find out if he'll be rejected or not. He figures if he asks your pal about you, she'll pass along the information and something may develop.

3. Making you laugh.

Is he cracking jokes around you constantly? Then he obviously likes you. He thinks if he can impress you with his antics, then you might just go out with him. Laughter is the best medicine, and all that.

4. Staring at you but not saying anything.

He's checking you out. You look away. When you look back up, he's still staring. Is he trying to hyp-notize you? Challenging you to a staring contest? No, he's just letting you know he's interested.

5. Telling you he likes your hair / outfit / nail polish.

Is he complimenting you on the littlest things? He likes you. First of all, he actually took the time to notice whatever it is he's complimenting you on. And guys aren't known for noticing things, okay? And the more minuscule the thing is, the more he likes you. Like if he comments on your lipstick shade, he's head over heels—no doubt about it.

6. Buying you a candy bar from the vending machine.

If he buys you something—even as small as a Snickers—he's into you! The logic being: If he gives you a sweet treat, you'll be sweet on him.

7. Telling you your boyfriend's a jerk.

When he's talking badly about your boyfriend or crush, that's boy-ese for "That guy's a jerk! You should be going out with a nice guy like me instead!" Good thing you're bilingual!

8. Offering to help you study.

Why does he care if you ace the Spanish final? Because he likes

you, that's why. And studying with you means he actually gets to spend time with you after school. His dream come true!

9. Telling you the dance is going to be "really lame."

If he tells you a particular event is going to suck, this is his way of seeing if you think it's going to blow, too, or if you might even want to go with—gulp—him. For example: Him: "This dance is going to be so stupid." You: "I don't think it's stupid—I think it's going to be kind of cool." Him: "Oh, you do? Well, yeah, maybe. Do you, ah, want to go with me?" See how easy it is?

10. Loitering by your locker.

If he's hanging by you in the halls with no apparent destination, he's into you. He likes you and wants to be near you in case you drop your books or something.

what kind of flirt are you?

1. You see a hot guy at a party. What's your next move?

    a) Slyly look over at him, then quickly look away

    b) Smile at him and make extended eye contact

    c) Walk up to him and tell him he's the cutest boy at the bash

2. It's the first day of school, and you can't help but notice a cute transfer student in first hour. What do you do?

    a) Sit over on his side of the room

    b) Introduce yourself

    c) Ask if he wants to join you for lunch

3. Your cousin introduces you to his best friend, an adorable aspiring actor you recognize from the Drama Club. You:

    a) look deep into his eyes and smile dazzlingly.

    b) casually ask how the school play is going.

    c) offer to be president of his first-ever fan club.

4. You're checking out a book in the library when the guy you've had a crush on forever gets in line directly behind you. What do you do?

    a) Look straight ahead and pretend you don't see him.

    b) Glance over your shoulder and give him a shy smile.

    c) Turn around and ask him what book he's checking out.

5. A gorgeous guy is checking you out at the mall. You:

    a) look down at your shoes.

    b) wave.

    c) laughingly ask him what he's staring at.

6. You're at the grocery store with Mom when you notice how cute the cashier is. How do you react?

    a) Blush profusely

    b) Ask him how his day's going

    c) Hand him a flier for a party your friend's throwing

7. You're walking the family pooch when a gorgeous guy comes along walking a golden retriever. You:

    a) grin, then keep walking.

    b) tell him what a cute dog he has.

    c) chat with him for a moment, then ask if he wants to walk together.

8. What do you typically do to get a hot guy's attention?

    a) Not much

    b) Just be yourself

    c) Anything and everything

9. A guy tells you he thinks you're cute. How do you respond?
   a) With a fit of giggles
   b) "Thank you!"
   c) "You're not so bad yourself!"

10. Your crush, who's sitting next to you in the cafeteria, has a big glob of ketchup on his cheek. What do you do?
   a) Say nothing and try to ignore it
   b) Hand him a napkin and tell him what's up
   c) Lean over and wipe it off for him

Figure out what your most popular response was—A, B, or C—to discover your flirting style.

Mostly A's: Super Shy

You're the kind of girl who would never go out of her way to overtly flirt with a guy—but that's what makes you so irresistible. Your stolen glances, flushed cheeks, and shy smiles are super-charming . . . and, more important, super-effective. Just make sure you do at least a little something to get his attention—or he just might slip away.

Mostly B's: Phenomenally Friendly

You're so at ease with the male species. You treat guys like you would treat anyone else—and this is what makes you so desirable. Your friendly demeanor and laid-back attitude make boys feel totally comfortable and secure. As long as the guy

you like treats you like a girl instead of "just one of the guys,"
you're in.

Mostly C's: Wonderfully Wild

Do you have guts or what? You'll do about anything to get a
guy's attention, no matter how brazen. Your charisma and charm
capture guys' hearts every time. But make sure you ditch the
wild-child act long enough for him to see the true you once in a
while, or else you'll shortchange yourself and your guy.

chapter 4

the dating game

I love that show *Blind Date*. You know, the one where they set people up on, uh, blind dates? It completely represents the real-life dating scene. Think about it. Sometimes the dates go really smoothly, like the couple is 100 percent meant for each other. Other times it's as if they can't stand the sight of each other. Isn't that how dating is? It can be so fun when everything goes smoothly. But when things are going horribly, the date can feel like a never-ending nightmare. Sometimes you can't even find out a boy is Mr. Wrong until you actually go out with him. And just how are you supposed to bail when you're smack-dab in the middle of an official date from hell? You'll find out in this chapter—as well as learn how to plan a great date, why you shouldn't date your best friend's ex, and scads more info I've learned after surviving hundreds of dates over the years. Here we go . . . .

Asking Him Out

Some old-fashioned girls (and the authors of *The Rules*) might disagree, but I say if you want to ask a guy out, you should go for it. After all, why the hell should you sit around waiting for your phone to ring when you could easily be the one to make things happen? I would have never even gone out once with my awesome hubby, Jay, if I hadn't asked him myself, because he later told me he was too freaked to ask me. So comprehend this: If I never had the guts to ask this guy out, I would not be married to him now. This is a fact. Not that you want to marry anyone at this point, but you could be depriving yourself of some major fun if you don't just bite the bullet and ask. Do it! The worst that can happen is that he says no—and that way you at least know for sure. Because if you don't ask him, you're getting a "no" anyway, right? So asking him increases your chances of getting a "yes" by about a million percent!

The way you actually go about asking him out is a delicate matter. As I explained in Chapter 2, I'm all for the casual invite, such as: "A bunch of us are going to that concert on Saturday. Wanna come?" That way, if he says no, he'll never know for sure if you were actually asking him out or just asking him as a friend. After all, it's a group outing. You might have asked fifty guys for all he knows.

If you want to pose the one-on-one invite, it's definitely riskier—but you only live once, right? Just ask him the way you would want to be asked. "Want to go to the movies on Friday night?" or any direct question will suffice. If you're nervous, you can always do the "friend background check" first. This is when you ask a friend of his if the guy would want to go out with you on Friday. A little wimpier, for sure, but at least you have an inkling of what his answer will be. I don't personally recommend this one because the friend could spread that you like him all over school or something equally horrific. It's best to go directly to the source. But you've got to know your options.

So once you ask the question, it's going to go one of three ways. He's either going to say yes, say no, or skirt the issue. If he says yes, it's a no-brainer: You just make your plans and go from there. If you get a no, just say, "That's cool," and walk off. Don't prolong the pain any longer than you have to. You could always say you were just kidding to save face, but this might look a little pathetic. Better to just stroll off with your head held high and a smile on your face. Because it's totally his loss. He is missing out on the best thing he'll ever have by saying no to you. Remember that! If he gives you some kind of absurd excuse or says he has to get back to you, smile and say, "Maybe another time, then," and walk off. I once had a guy tell me he couldn't go to a Chainsaw Kittens concert with me because his "grandma might be visiting, maybe." Whatever! Obviously he didn't have the balls to say no to me, but that was his problem. I went to the concert anyway and had an awesome time. If he's turning you down in a roundabout way, don't wait for him to clarify. Just move on. He's not worth your time!

Being Asked Out

If you don't ask them out, your dates obviously have to ask you out. If every guy who ever asked you out was someone you were dying to go out with, this would be great. But chances are that some of the time, the guy doing the asking isn't exactly dreamboat material. What to do?

Be as direct as possible without hurting his feelings. If you like him and want to go out, say yes (obviously). But if he's someone you're not sure you like enough to date, take a moment to ponder before you respond. Do you think you'll have fun with this guy? Is he someone you could even remotely see yourself dating? If the answer is yes, you might as well go out with him at least once. You might be pleasantly surprised. But if he's someone that you no-way-in-hell would ever want to spend an evening with, just say no. Making a lame excuse could easily lead him to believe you like him, and will also more than likely lead to another date invite. If you're not comfortable saying the N-word, simply say you just got out of a relationship and are taking a time-out right now. This way he won't take it personally—but will definitely get the message that you're not into dating at the moment. If you're pals with the guy already, saying you don't want to jeopardize your friendship is always a good one. This way, you're not dating him to "save the friendship." He can't argue with that one, can he?

Being Set Up

The other, albeit more rocky, road to romance is the "setup." Maybe your friend's boyfriend has a friend he wants you to meet. Or so-and-so's cousin is in town and wants to get together. Whatever the circumstances, it's a blind date. And deciding whether or not to agree to one is a slippery situation indeed.

If you do go, you're taking a risk—and risks are good. It's like buying a lottery ticket. He might be totally boring, sure, but then again he might not. And if you don't like him, at least you'll have an amusing story to share with your friends. I used to keep a "Dates from Hell" journal to record my less-desirable dating adventures. Try it—it's fun!

If you agree to a blind date, just give yourself over to the fact that it's an awkward situation and that your date is probably feeling just as freaked. Since you don't know each other at all, you can ask each other all sorts of weird and interesting questions. Get creative. Find out who his first crush was and what his least-favorite food is. Pretend you're Oprah and he's your guest. Have fun with it. I mean, why the hell not?

The Age Game

If you're considering dating an older or younger guy, there are certain things to consider. First, is the age gap so big that it's going to be a problem? A couple of years shouldn't make that big of a difference. But if he's seven years older than you are, you're obviously going to be in different universes. If you met a thirty-four-year-old when you were twenty-seven, that wouldn't be so drastic, but the difference between seventeen and twenty-four is like dog years. The typical twenty-four-year-old is out of college already and starting his career. A seventeen-year-old is still thinking about stuff like the prom. Different worlds.

Same goes for dating someone younger. A year or two is no big deal, but do you really want to go out with a guy who's smack-dab in the middle of puberty when you're filling out college applications? Girls are more mature than guys anyway, so dating someone way younger is going to make you feel like you're dating a grade schooler. You've got to use your own judgment, of course, but think about it before you dive into anything. The odds are definitely stacked against you.

First-Date Do's and Don'ts

You've got a date. It's official. Now what?

First, don't freak out about it. The more you stress over a

date, the less relaxed you'll be—and that's not going to be good for anybody. The reason you're going out is because you like each other's company and want to get to know each other a little bit more. No one's expecting you to be perfect or look like Miss America here. You want to be yourself.

I know, I know—I can hear the groans from here. You've heard that one a million times, right? "Be yourself! Be yourself!" I remember my eyes used to roll like roulette wheels when I heard that one. But, like many clichés, this one is repeated over and over because it's actually true. You don't have to kill yourself trying to be someone you're not to impress a date. Really. Because in the end you want him to like you for you, right? Well, how can he fall for the real you if he never gets a chance to meet her?

Case in point: I once was in love with this guy named Clark. Totally head over heels for this guy, I'm not kidding. So I heard that he liked the band the Cure. Next thing you know, I'm telling him that I love that band, even though I'm not into them at all. I then proceed to head to the nearest record store and buy every single one of their CDs. I listened to them nonstop after that, even though I couldn't stand their music. I wanted to have something in common with Clark. But now that I'm older and a little wiser, I can see how truly pitiful that was. Guys don't want clones of themselves. They want girls with their own interests and opinions, likes and dislikes. He would have probably liked me way more if I'd said, "Oh—I'm not really into them. I love the Dixie Chicks." Then he could have shown me what he thought was cool about the Cure and I could have shown him why I thought the Dixie Chicks ruled. But instead I tried to be someone I wasn't and never let him in on the things that truly make me me. You know what I mean?

So we've got the "be yourself" rule down. Good. Now, on to the next one—what to wear. Again, I say wear whatever you normally would. You don't want to depart from your normal style just to impress him. I remember when my friend Staci started dating this hip-hop guy and she totally dressed the part—all baggy jeans and big shirts, the whole nine yards. Her entire life she had been Miss Preppy USA, so it was pretty hilarious. But at the end of the relationship she had a whole new wardrobe of clothes she would never, ever wear again. The reason she'd even bought them in the first place was to impress some guy. It's not worth it. Seriously.

Another thing to remember on a first date: Do not, under any circumstances, tell the guy your whole life story. You want to preserve a little mystery here, and if you tell him everything about yourself, what will you talk about on your second date? Do you really want someone you barely know to know everything about you? And, on that note, do not talk about your ex-boyfriends. I once spent two hours telling a guy I hardly knew all the reasons why my ex-boyfriend sucked. And guess what? He never called me again. Guys don't want to hear about other guys you've gone out with. I think my twisted logic at the time was that if he heard all about my ex and how many other guys I'd gone out with, he'd see that I was super-desirable and had gone out with lots of people—he was lucky to be out with me! Instead, I was just showing him that I had no boundaries and wasn't exactly over my ex yet. And that I was maybe just a little bit whacked. Not exactly the message I was hoping to send out, obviously.

And, finally, instead of stressing out about whether he likes you, think about whether or not you like him. A lot of times girls focus so much on whether or not the guy likes them, they don't even bother thinking about whether they like him. I've definitely done this in the past. But your opinion counts just as much as his does! Are you with him because he's the boy for you or simply because he's a boy? You're cheating yourself if you're dating him just to be dating someone. Remember: It's hard to meet Mr. Right when you're with Mr. Right-for-Now!

Dates That Rate

Are you sick to death of going on boring dates? Tired of the usual food-and-flicks fare? I feel your pain. After enduring one too many nondescript nights of my own, I decided enough was enough. Here, ten dates guaranteed to transform your love life from yawn-inspiring to awe-inspiring.

1. Star Light, Star Bright

 Remember busing over to the planetarium during your field-trip days? Although its romance was lost on you as a grade schooler, it's never too late to make up for lost time. Stargazing with your sweetie in a dark auditorium—low music humming in the background, head resting on his shoulder—is out of this world!

2. And Bingo Was His Name-O

Longing for a cozy table for two, sumptuous snack-bar delicacies, plus a chance to win a big chunk of change? Look no further than your nearest bingo parlor. The players: you, your man, and your lucky rabbit's foot. When the announcer calls, "B-9," your Bingo Boy will be thinking, Be mine!

3. Ice, Ice Baby

Even if it's the dog days of summer, you
and your man can still create your own
winter wonderland at the local ice-skating
rink. Picture this: You're Tara Lipinski in
your rockin' rink skirt, sipping steaming
hot chocolate and doing figure eights.

Bonus: gives you an excellent excuse to "accidentally" fall onto
your date—then watch him fall for you in a major way.

4. On the Move

You're starving but don't want to do the pizza parlor scene with
everybody else and their dog. Why not suggest a rotating dinner?
Eat appetizers at one spot, the main course at another, and
dessert at a third. You'll experience new places, faces, and fla-
vors as you restaurant-hop around the city. Dinner doesn't have
to equal dud.

5. Let the Sun Go Down on Me

If you're in the mood for romance, check out
the sun's disappearing act. Here's the plan:
Go to a secluded area armed with a picnic
basket full of nonalcoholic champagne,
strawberries, and a fuzzy blanket. Tell your date you
read somewhere that it's good luck to kiss at the exact moment
the sun goes down. You can thank me later.

6. The Big Splash

Up for some *Baywatch* action? If so, take a dip with your date—in a hotel swimming pool. Wear swimsuits (under your clothes, silly) and stroll into the hotel as confidently as VIP guests. Ride the elevator to the floor of your choice to avoid suspicion, then head straight back down to the pool. Bring along two fresh towels and an inflatable inner tube in a tote and you're golden. Surf's up, Moondoggie!

7. Hole in One

When you're jonesing for adventure Tiger Woods–style, look no further than the miniature golf course. Ask your man for some help with your swing and—voilà!—suddenly you're in his arms. To make the game even more interesting, make a bet: Whoever wins buys the loser a postgame hot-fudge sundae.

8. A League of Their Own

Popcorn, hot dogs, and home-team pride take on a whole new meaning when you're watching pint-sized players round the bases. So go ahead—find a Little League game, park your butts on the bleachers, and scream for the kids with the coolest uniforms.

9. Eye on the Sky

Checking out the arriving and departing planes from your airport's observation deck can equal off-the-charts romance. Dish about dream vacations and get friendly with your fellow while scoping out the sky-high activity, then stop by the snack bar for some airport eats.

10. License to Drive

If you must have a movie date, the drive-in is the only way to go. Stock your car with snacks, a cooler full of drinks, and your favorite tapes for intermission-listenin'. As you lay your head on his shoulder while the images flicker on the screen, you'll feel positively retro!

"Biggie" Dates

Certain dates—like the prom and Homecoming—are more important than others. Going to an event like this with someone is major. It's basically your version of the Academy Awards, right? And there are certain expectations, shall we say, attached to attending an event of this magnitude with a guy. First of all, there's a lot of money being spent on an evening like this, and some jerks think they should get a return on their investment. You do not owe the guy anything in the booty department just for taking you to a dance, and he's way off if he tries to convince you otherwise. (If you're in love and want to seal the deal, read Chapter 7 before making any decisions.) Other girls think if they aren't asked to the dance, they should just sit home and rot. No way! I say you should go with your friends and have fun. Or ask someone yourself. You only live once. Make it count!

is he second-date material?

1. When he picked you up for the date, how prompt was he?
- a) A little early or right on time
- b) Five minutes late
- c) More than five minutes late

2. How did you decide what to do on the date?
- a) You both decided.
- b) He decided without asking you.
- c) You decided.

3. If you went out to eat, how would you rate his table manners on a scale of one to ten?
- a) Top-notch (8–10)
- b) So-so (4–7)
- c) Lousy (1–3)

4. During the date, what did you talk about?
- a) He mainly asked you questions.
- b) You chatted about both of your interests.
- c) Three topics: him, him, and him

5. When you were speaking, did he really listen?

    a) He hung on to your every word.

    b) He seemed pretty interested.

    c) Well, he did interrupt you several times . . . .

6. Who paid?

    a) He did.

    b) You went Dutch.

    c) You did.

7. If you ran into his friends during the outing, what did your date do? (If you didn't, give yourself three points.)

    a) Introduced you to them

    b) Talked to them for a second, then focused his attention back on you

    c) Chatted with them at length and ignored you

8. If you went to a movie on the date, who chose the flick?

    a) You did.

    b) You both did.

    c) He did.

9. As far as getting physical was concerned, what was his motto?

    a) Won't take no for an answer

    b) Perfect gentleman

    c) A little handsy, but that was okay

10. When he took you home, he got you there:

    a) on time.

    b) late.

    c) early.

Scoring:

1. a) 3; b) 2; c) 1	**6.** a) 3; b) 2; c) 1
2. a) 2; b) 1; c) 3	**7.** a) 3; b) 2; c) 1
3. a) 3; b) 2; c) 1	**8.** a) 3; b) 2; c) 1
4. a) 3; b) 2; c) 1	**9.** a) 1; b) 3; c) 2
5. a) 3; b) 2; c) 1	**10.** a) 3; b) 1; c) 2

Should you go out with him again? Add up your score to find out.

10–16: No Way, José

This guy's a jerk with a capital J. Not only should you not grant him a second date, he didn't even deserve a first! Kick him to the curb. You could do so much better!

17–23: Maybe, Baby

Sure, there were a few rough patches in your outing, but this guy definitely had his good points. If you have any desire to see him again, go for it. He's worth a second chance.

24–30: Yessiree, Bob

What a sweetie! This guy's a first-rate date who's got all the right moves and a heart of gold. (Corny, but true.) Run, don't walk, to your second date with this guy. He's a find.

bad behavior

In a perfect world, boys would always be sweet and loving and super-supportive. But in the real world (and we're not talking MTV here), guys can sometimes be real jerks. What girl doesn't have a horror story about a guy not calling her back, standing her up for a date, or doing something equally offensive? I've certainly met up with my share of assholes, and I'm sure you have, too. The next couple of pages will help you cope when he tries to tell you what to do, feeds you ridiculous excuses, or makes out with another girl. And we'll deal with more serious stuff like date rape and physical abuse, too. You don't have to put up with being treated this way. You really don't. Need more proof? Get ready . . . .

The Blow-Off

Every guy has done it. Acts interested in you, like he just can't wait to rent movies on Saturday night. Says he'll be at your place at 7:30 sharp. Well, 7:30 comes and he's not there. 7:40, 7:50. And suddenly it's 9:00 and you realize you've been sitting there for an hour and a half without so much as a phone call. If you do get mad enough to call him, chances are he's not home. He's "out." And no, his mom doesn't know when he'll be back. Do you want to leave a message? Sure, but the kind of message you want to leave isn't exactly suitable for good ol' Mom to hear. Urgh! Why do boys do this? I'm not sure. I have asked several and gotten a variety of responses, from "Sometimes I forget the plans I make" (hello, just write it down, right?) to "Well, I had a better offer" (what a loser!). So even though I don't know exactly why he's blowing you off, I can help you figure out how to deal.

If he says he's going to call at a certain time and doesn't, give him a fifteen-minute grace period, then leave. Go to your best friend's house. Go to the store with your mom. Go ride your bike. Do anything—but don't sit by that phone. I guess in theory you could do something at home, like surf the 'Net or watch TV, but you'd still subconsciously be listening for that phone to ring. My advice is: Get out. Even if it's just a walk around the block, leave the premises. And if he does call while you're gone, let him get the machine and wonder where you are. Because that's the kind of girl you are—someone who doesn't wait for the phone to ring.

If he was supposed to pick you up for a date and doesn't show up, again—give him a thirty-minute grace period. Then bail. If you're thinking about calling his house to make sure he wasn't in a car wreck or something (because we always think there's got to be a reason, right?), think again. The guys I surveyed said a call makes you look desperate. Better just to get out of there. Go over to a pal's, to a movie, anywhere. If he does end up calling, instruct whoever's home to tell him you got sick of waiting and made alternate plans. If there was some kind of mixup, I swear he'll understand. Because guys respect a girl with a backbone. You're the kind of girl who has better things to do with your time than wait around for his late butt to pick you up. You've got places to go, people to see. You're busy. And as my favorite boy in the world always says, "Busy is attractive!"

But what if he does apologize profusely after blowing you off and promises never, ever to do it again? If you really like the guy, go ahead and give him three strikes to avoid any regrets. But on the third strike, he's out. Don't give him five or six or ten, because you're worth more than that. You deserve someone who's going to respect you and your time. If he can't do that, then it's over. Period.

The Lying Game

Sometimes guys lie. And certain guys lie way more than others. Over stupid stuff—like where they've been, who they were talking to, even what they ate for breakfast. Why do they do this? There are a variety of possibilities: (a) They are trying to impress you; (b) they think the truth will make you mad so they lie to you instead; (c) they are pathological liars who fib for no reason; or (d) they think it's funny to lie to you and see if you'll believe them. My opinion is: If you can't believe what your guy tells you, you don't have much of a relationship. Because a relationship has to be built on trust, and how can you trust someone who lies to you? You can't.

And I'm not talking about little white lies, either. If he asks you if you like his shirt and you tell him yes to spare his feelings, that's obviously not in the same category as him telling you he was tending to his sick grandpa when he was actually out with another girl. You know the difference.

Let's say he told you a lie. A biggie. And you found out for sure he wasn't telling the truth. You've got to call him on it. If he denies it, tell him you're not as stupid or gullible as he might think you are. If you have proof he's lying, that's all the better. Force him to admit he's lying, if possible. Some guys will never admit it, though. But if he does fess up, ask him why he's doing it.

Again, there are a million different responses you might receive at this point. He thought the truth would hurt you, he didn't want to make you cry, he actually thought he was doing you a favor by not telling you the whole story. Whatever. At this stage, you have to make it clear that you will not tolerate someone telling you lies. Be firm. Tell him that when he lies to you, it pretty much erases any kind of trust the two of you share. And tell him that if he does it one more time, he's out.

This is where the hard part comes in. If he actually does lie to you one more time (and he probably will), you have to make good on your word. If you told him he was going to get the boot, then the boot is what you have to give him. Because if you don't, your word doesn't mean much, either.

I know it's hard, especially if you really like the guy. But if you can't believe a word he says, how bright is your future? One of my exes constantly lied about the stupidest stuff: that he was third in the world in windsurfing, he'd been a Navy SEAL, his band had a video on MTV. I mean, give me a break. It was ridiculous. And finally it just had to end. Because he was never going to stop lying. And I was never going to start believing him. So we were at a dead end.

You deserve to be with someone who is going to tell you the truth. And you deserve someone you can believe in. Give yourself the chance to find that person.

His Cheating Heart

You're dating him. Everything's going great. Then you hear through the grapevine that he made out with Susie from Home

Ec on Friday night. What? You're shocked. Flabbergasted. You ask him about it. He admits that he kissed her but insists it didn't mean anything. Well, maybe it didn't mean anything to him, but it certainly means something to you. You're hurt, upset, embarrassed, humiliated. He begs your forgiveness. It was a mistake, he says, and he promises it will never happen again. What are you supposed to do?

It depends how strongly you feel about it. We all have different values and lists of what we can and can't deal with. You could think, "If he cheats on me, it's over." And so when he kissed Susie Friday night, he effectively ended the relationship. You tell him so and never look back.

But your internal rule might be something along the lines of "If he sleeps with someone else, it's over." And since he didn't technically sleep with Susie—they just kissed—you can see taking him back.

My advice is to follow your heart here. If you don't want to take him back and feel you can never trust him again, end it. If you do want to give him one more chance, make it clear that if he does something like this again, it's over. And stick to your guns. Because you don't deserve to be with a guy who kisses other girls. Your guy should be so into you that he can't even imagine kissing someone else. Because you rule! Don't forget that.

Let's Get Serious

The next few categories are way more serious than lying or cheating. In fact, some of these behaviors are even life-threatening. I wish I didn't have to include this in a "fun" guide for girls, but the fact is that there are some bad guys out there who will put you in bad situations. And if you have the misfortune of getting involved with one of them, you need the skills to survive. Knowledge is power. Ideally, you won't have to use the following advice at any point in your life because all of your dates will be sweet and loving and trustworthy. But if you do find yourself in a dangerous situation, I hope these words will pop up in your brain and help you get out.

Substance Abuse

If he drinks or does drugs on your dates, this is obviously bad news. Again, there are different levels here. A guy drinking one Bud Light is not the same as a guy shooting up heroin. But if he is doing something that is making you uncomfortable, it's not cool. And if that behavior is putting you in any danger of any kind, it's unacceptable.

If he's drinking around you at a party, only you know what you're willing to put up with. But DO NOT under any circumstances get in a car with someone who has been drinking. Even if you've drunk more than he has or you think he's okay to drive, don't get in the car. Bum a ride with someone sober, call a cab, walk home (if it's close enough), or call your parents and tell them the situation. They might be upset, sure, but deep down they'll respect you for calling them instead of getting in a car with someone who's drunk. You might even consider talking to your parents hypothetically about what you should do if you're dating someone who's been drinking and you don't want to get in the car with him. Chances are they'll tell you to call them at any time, day or night. My mom gave me fifty cents to tape to the back of my license—that way I'd always have change for the pay phone if I needed to call her for a ride.

And the same advice goes for dating someone who's been doing drugs. Don't get in the car with him. You might think nothing will happen, but something very well could. Don't risk your life for this guy—no guy is worth that.

Another thing to consider when you're dating someone who's doing drugs is that you could get arrested if you get pulled over and he has drugs. My friend Jill's parents got arrested for running a drug house when her boyfriend grew marijuana in their basement (without their knowledge, no less). You can imagine how well that went over. And her boyfriend actually went to jail for nine months. This is serious stuff. Don't screw up your future!

Here's another bit of info I've unfortunately learned from experience: When a guy is wasted, he's not on your wavelength.

And you end up either baby-sitting him or tolerating his infantile antics for the entire evening. My first boyfriend, Nathan, used to drink a twelve-pack every single night. I thought it was no big deal at first. But pretty soon he moved on to marijuana and began blowing me off for his bong. We even stopped kissing. I was totally alone, even though I had a boyfriend. No, correction, I was worse than alone, because I was cleaning up his vomit from my front seat and putting up with him and his friends getting plastered on our supposed "dates." Was it worth it? No, of course not. But I did learn something, albeit the hard way: Just because a boy needs you doesn't mean he loves you. There's a big difference. And you can't be his mom and his girlfriend at the same time. And when you're dating a substance abuser, you invariably become his mom—making sure he turns in his assignments on time, driving him around (since he's too drunk), and picking up after his wasted self. He needs to get his life together before he can be the boyfriend you want him to be. I loved Nathan, but love wasn't enough. And it won't be enough with your guy. You can't change him. The sooner you accept that, the sooner you can move on.

Date Rape

We delve into the whole sex issue in Chapter 7 (page 129), but one thing I definitely want to address in "Bad Behavior" is date rape. No guy has the right to tell you what to do with your body. And no matter how much money he spent on you during your outing, this doesn't give him an all-access pass to your private parts.

In Canada and the United States, 1.3 women are raped every minute. That results in 78 rapes each hour, 1,872 rapes each day, 56,160 rapes each month, and 683,280 rapes each year. And cases reported to law enforcement show that 70 to 80 percent of all rapes are acquaintance or date rapes. That's a scary statistic. And what's even more scary is that many people seem to think that if a girl drinks on a date or even wears a short skirt, she's "asking for it." That's ridiculous. No one deserves to be raped!

Others feel that if you were making out or messing around with the guy, that means you agreed to have sex with him. No means no—no matter how far you have gone with the guy before you say it. If he doesn't take no for an answer, it's rape.

If you do think you have been a victim of date rape, please tell someone—a trusted friend, a parent, a teacher. Or call RAINN, the Rape, Abuse, and Incest National Network Hotline, at 1-800-656-HOPE. What happened to you is against the law, and there is help available. The sooner you report him, the better.

Although there is nothing you can do to 100 percent guarantee you never get date-raped, there are some precautions you can take. Take kick-boxing or self-defense classes to build up your muscles and your confidence. Since drugs and alcohol break down your defenses and decrease your ability to take care of yourself, watch your intake to avoid putting yourself in a dangerous position. And trust your instincts. If a guy takes you somewhere that makes you feel uneasy or starts acting strange, get out. If you don't know him that well, meet in a public place for your date (like the movies or the mall) rather than letting him pick you up. That way you're not in the car alone with him. And do not, under any circumstances, leave a party or a club with a guy you just met or don't know very well. I have done it myself, and now I realize how lucky I was. The guys could have been ax murderers for all I knew, and a lot of times I had been drinking when I got in the guy's car. Don't be as dumb as I was! Protect yourself. You are your own greatest defender.

Emotional Abuse

Guys who call you names or put you down constantly may not be hitting you, but they are abusing you. One of the biggest perpetrators of emotional abuse are control freaks. We've all met a few. Guys who tell you how much makeup to put on. Or which dress you should wear. How many times a day you should call him. What you should say and when you should say it. When and where you should see your friends—if he "lets" you see them at all. I don't know where these guys get off. Maybe their dads were like this and they're just repeating the pattern. But you do not, I repeat DO NOT, have to put up with it.

The bottom line is: He's your boyfriend, not your boss. He has no right to tell you what to do. If you notice that he's starting to make demands, tell him straight-up that you're not going to take orders from him. Give him one more chance if you must. And if he does it again, end it. Again, I realize this is really hard to do, especially if you like the guy, but you do not need someone who controls you. This is abuse. And he'll make your life hell. You are your own person with your own brain and your own ideas. You don't need someone to tell you how to live your life. You can live your own life. And the life you lead will be a lot happier without someone like him in it.

THE PICTURE TRICK

If you're having a hard time telling your abuser to hit the road, look at a picture of yourself at age five or six. Would you let this guy treat this little girl that way? Because you are still that little girl on the inside. Protect her from this monster. Get help.

Then there are the guys who call you a "bitch" or "whore." Tell you you're worthless. Stupid. Ugly. Fat. Each word is like a little knife, jabbing away at your self-esteem and your soul. And you know what happens if you listen to him long enough? You start to believe it. My alcoholic boyfriend (who also tended to be emotionally abusive) told me I was "nothing." I, a person who was so full of life and cool and cute and had everything going for me except for my bad choice in guys, was "nothing." And you know what? I felt like nothing when we broke up. Because I had no friends—he didn't like my friends, so I rarely saw them. I had no life, since I'd made my boyfriend my whole life. And I had no self-worth. I had to start from ground zero. Don't let these losers dictate what you think about yourself. Don't give them that power. You rule and you know you rule! You're the best! And don't let some jerk tell you otherwise. Cut him loose before his rude rantings and ravings become your own internal monologue. Because they will. It'll become a jingle you can't get out of your head, no matter how hard you try. Don't let him do that to you. Someone who really loved you would never talk to you that way. The kind of boyfriend you deserve is someone who will tell you you're awesome and the most amazing girl on the planet. Because you are. You are.

Physical Abuse

Many emotionally abusive guys are also physically abusive. The thought of one of these jerks actually hitting his girlfriend makes me sick to my stomach, but it's a reality. You don't have to put up with it. It's against the law. And a guy who loved you would never show it with his fists. No matter what.

Let me tell you what happens after he hits you the first time. He brings you a present or sends you flowers. Cries. Says he's sorry. Promises it will never happen again. But then something sets him off and he does do it again—only this time it's worse. Then come bigger presents and bigger sobs and bigger I'm sorrys. And next thing you know he puts you in the hospital

NEED HELP? TEN THINGS YOU CAN DO RIGHT NOW

1. Report him to the police.
2. Don't be alone with him.
3. Tell your parents.
4. Tell someone—anyone—what this guy is doing to you.
5. Call a national hotline.
6. Tell him in no uncertain terms that you never want to see him again.
7. Join a support group.
8. Let your family pamper and love you.
9. Tell your friends.
10. Confide in a school counselor.

with a broken bone. Or he's bringing you flowers to your gravesite.

Is this how you want your life to play out—like a bad Movie of the Week? You've got to stop him. Do it today. If he hits you, get out of there. Take yourself out of danger. Tell him it's over. And he doesn't even necessarily have to hit you. He could shove you, slap you, knock you down, pull your hair. Whatever it is that he's doing, put a stop to it today. Tell somebody. Even if you love him, love yourself more. Because this guy needs to be punished. And he needs help. You don't deserve to be treated this way. You don't, no matter how much he tries to convince you it's your fault. If you don't feel comfortable telling a friend or parent, call the National Domestic Violence Hotline at 1-800-333-SAFE. If you can't do it for yourself, do it for me. I care!

Follow Me

Sometimes a guy can't get the hint that you don't like him. Maybe you went on a date with him and it didn't work out. Maybe you even had a relationship. Or maybe you barely know the guy at all. But suddenly you start getting notes. Phone calls. You start seeing him everywhere. Wherever you go, he's there. He's following you. You try to tell yourself that it's no big deal, but it is a big deal. He's stalking you, which is against the law. And it's putting you in a dangerous position.

Don't respond to any of his messages or try to talk some

sense into him. This just feeds his obsession. And no amount of reasoning is going to make him see the light. You've got to tell someone—a parent, school counselor, friend. Or report him to authorities. Get a restraining order. If you feel you're in immediate danger, call 911. You don't have to put up with this. Don't let a psycho like this control your life. Take back the control. Take charge!

The Morning After

I'm going to assume that you've taken all of my advice and are no longer putting up with any bad behavior. Congratulations! Either one of two things has happened: He's changed or he's gone. If your guy has shaped up, that's great. But if he lapses back into his old patterns, let him know you won't put up with it. Be strong.

If you were forced to break up with him, you've done yourself a favor. I know it's hard. Go directly to Chapter 12 (page 203) for a crash-course on life without him. Because, even when people treat us badly, that doesn't mean we didn't love them. And it doesn't mean that losing them doesn't hurt. Because it does.

But you have done what you had to do. He was treating you badly. You didn't deserve it. You had no other choice. And it's his loss.

Why You Stay

Any of this sound familiar? Below, the five top reasons girls stay, along with five reasons why they shouldn't.

1. "I can change him."

No, you can't. Because no one can change him if he doesn't want to change himself. And with the major problems he has, it's probably going to take a professional to straighten him out. Don't fight a losing battle.

2. "He was so sweet in the beginning."

Every guy is on his best behavior in the beginning. Is he going to hit you on the first date? Or call you a slut? You'd never go out with him again. Instead, he wins you over with his false self, then lets his true self come out after you're fooled. If you're waiting for him to turn back into the guy you fell in love with, it's never going to happen. Because that isn't who he truly is. This is.

3. "He says he loves me."

Talk is cheap, and actions speak louder than words. He might say he loves you, but how does he treat you? Because love isn't just something people say, it's something they do. Is he showing you he loves you by treating you this way? Quite the opposite.

4. "We've been together so long."

I've been guilty of this one. You've been with him for a year and a half, so you can't break up with him now. All that time would be wasted. But what if you were told your car had major engine damage and could blow up at any minute? Would you still drive it, just because you've had it over a year? No, you'd get rid of it because it's dangerous. And that's what you need to do here.

5. "I'm scared to be alone."

It is scary being alone, especially if you're used to having a boyfriend. (See Chapter 12). But being solo is better than being with a guy who treats you like dirt. When you're single, you can do anything you want and don't have to put up with his B.S. It's not loneliness, it's freedom. You can do it!

Quiz

how does your man treat you?

1. You're wearing a new pair of Levi's when you decide to pop that age-old question: "Do I look fat?" He says:

    a) "Your butt's so big, it has its own zip code!"

    b) "Uh, you look fine."

    c) "No way! You're the most beautiful girl in the world!"

2. You're watching TV. You want to watch *Buffy*, he wants to watch MTV. Who wins?

    a) He does, as always.

    b) You decide to watch MTV and tape *Buffy*.

    c) You do—nothing comes between you and your *Buffy*!

3. You have plans to go to the movies with your b-friend. Right before you're supposed to go, his buddies invite him to go out. He:

    a) blows you off to hang with his friends.

    b) asks if you can go to a later movie, then meets up with the guys first.

    c) tells his buds he's already got plans.

4. You want to go out with your gal pals on Saturday night. How does he react?

    a) He asks why you feel the need to go out without him, then broods till you cancel.

    b) He pouts for a bit, then finally seems cool with it.

    c) He's all for it—and even plans a Boys' Night Out for that same evening.

5. Your boyfriend sees you talking to a guy from your French class. What does he do?

    a) Accuses you of cheating on him

    b) Asks what you guys were talking about

    c) Doesn't say a thing about it

6. If your boyfriend says he's going to call you at a certain time, does he?

    a) Nope—he's usually late, if he even calls at all.

    b) Sometimes he's a tad tardy.

    c) Of course he does!

7. Your b-friend asks you to pick him up a Big Gulp on your way over to his house. You totally space out and forget. He:

    a) totally freaks out, calling you stupid and clueless.

    b) acts pissed but eventually gets over it.

    c) hugs you and tells you it's no big deal.

8. You don't want to have sex and he does. Now what?

    a) He pressures you into it.

    b) He gripes about it but finally chills.

    c) He lets you call the shots.

9. You're wearing a halter top that totally shows off your curves. What's your man's fashion review?

    a) He tells you that it looks trashy and demands that you change.

    b) He raises his eyebrows but says nothing.

    c) He tells you that you look totally gorgeous.

10. You're walking down the hall when you accidentally trip and fall, sending your books flying. What does your b-friend do?

    a) Laughs hysterically at your clumsiness and doesn't even attempt to help you up

    b) Chuckles before offering you a hand

    c) Immediately gasps and asks if you're okay

Tally up your A's, B's, and C's, then see exactly how you're being treated by your man.

Mostly A's: Doormat City

This guy doesn't deserve a cool girl like you! He's rude, jealous, controlling, and an all-around bad boyfriend. You deserve so much better! Unless he gets a personality transplant, you need to lose this loser. You can't change him unless he wants to change himself. Do yourself a favor and quit while you're ahead!

Mostly B's: Mixed Signals

This guy's like Jekyll and Hyde. He can be sweet at times, but totally mean at others. Encourage him when he's treating you how you want to be treated and call him on it when he's not. If he acknowledges his bad behavior, then maybe that means he can change it. Together, you just might make it work. But if you can't, say good-bye with no regrets.

Mostly C's: Like a Princess

Where did you find this one? He treats you so great—trusting you completely, showering you with affection, and just basically being an all-around good guy. This is the kind of boyfriend that everybody's after—and, trust me, they're few and far between. As long as this guy continues to stay on good behavior, he's a true gem.

chapter 6

getting serious

O nce you date someone for a while, one of two things will happen: It will fizzle out or get serious. If your relationship is leaning toward the latter, I'm sure you're feeling all sorts of emotions. Happy you've found someone you like (or even love!!!!) this much, but scared what will happen once you take things a step further. It's uncharted territory, and you have every reason to feel scared, elated, excited, and terrified—or all of the above! I'm hoping your fears will subside after reading the following info. You'll learn how to decide when (or if) to become boyfriend-girlfriend, whether or not to say the L-word first, just exactly what that class ring symbolizes, and more. On your mark, get set . . .

Are We an Item or What?

You've been hanging out with him for some time. Weeks, maybe even months. But you're not sure if he's technically your boyfriend or not. I mean, you've never really called him that—out loud anyway. And since you've never discussed how serious you really are, you don't know how to react if another guy asks you out. Even worse, you don't know how he's reacting if another girl is making the moves on him. What do you do?

Consider how long you've been together. Have you been on more than nine dates? If not, it's probably too soon to bring up the seriousness issue. (That is, if you haven't had sex yet. If you have, proceed directly to "Sex and Seriousness," below. Do not pass go, do not collect $200.) If you are indeed in double-digit territory, things are probably starting to heat up. You're calling each other for no reason. Maybe even automatically assuming you'll see each other on Saturday nights without asking in advance. Sound familiar? If so, it appears that you're in an actual relationship. You've progressed past the "hanging out" stage and are now entering official "boyfriend-girlfriend" territory. But how do you go about calling him your boyfriend for the first time—especially in front of him, and even more especially if he hasn't called you his girlfriend yet? Well, it's touchy. There are a few ways to go about it.

First, you can just ask. Once I asked this guy I was totally in love with, "So, do you want to be my boyfriend?" and thankfully he said yes. I definitely had to psyche myself up for it, but we'd been going out for about two months and I already considered him my boyfriend in my heart—I just hadn't said it out loud yet. Or you could always do what my friend does, and just introduce him as your boyfriend to someone and see how

he reacts. One word of warning: Don't do this unless you're 99 percent sure he's as serious as you are. Another friend of mine introduced a guy as her boyfriend to her mom and the guy said, "Boyfriend? I'm not your boyfriend!" Talk about total mortification! She did survive, of course, but believe me, she had to be practically married from then on to refer to anyone as her b-friend. Lastly, you could simply wait for him to bring it up. I'm not a big fan of waiting, because I'm a take-action kind of girl. But this is definitely the safest option. If he calls you his girlfriend first, you can obviously call him your boyfriend whenever you want, and the pressure's off.

Once he's officially your boyfriend, there are a few things you must discuss. What does being a boyfriend mean to him? And what does being a girlfriend mean to you? He might think

TEN TOP SIGNS
HE'S GETTING SERIOUS

1. He knows your telephone number by heart.

2. He lets you wear his favorite sweatshirt.

3. He refers to you and himself as "we."

4. He puts you on his speed dial.

5. He knows what your favorite pizza is without having to ask.

6. He has a picture of you in his wallet.

7. He calls you first when he has big news.

8. He remembers the exact date of your first kiss.

9. He knows your cat's name.

10. He tells you his locker combination.

being your boyfriend means he sees you on weekends but can go out with anyone else he wants during the week. Or you might think being his girlfriend means that you see each other three nights a week, when he wants to be together 24/7. You've got to talk these things out. But this doesn't mean you have to call a meeting or anything. Just ask him over pizza what he wants out of the relationship, then tell him what you want out of it and compare notes. Communication is key here. As they say: You've got to name it to claim it!

Sex and Seriousness

Some people equate getting serious with having sex, but that's not necessarily the case. That's why I want to preface this by saying that if he's not your official boyfriend, I don't even consider him worth having sex with. It won't mean a thing if you don't have deep feelings for the guy, and how can you have deep feelings for someone you barely know? I don't want to be a hypocrite here. I have hooked up with a few guys I barely knew in the past, and that's why I can honestly say it SUCKS. Both of my nonboyfriend sexual experiences (one was a one-night stand; the other was this two-week fling) were completely lame and left me feeling very empty. Plus, casual sex is very dangerous. I don't even have to tell you how important it is to use condoms and all that, right? Before I start going on for pages and pages (because there's lots to say), let me just tell you that I get way more into this in the next chapter (page 129). So look for the juiciest details there.

As far as getting serious goes, you don't have to have sex to get serious. And you don't have to have sex to make him your boyfriend. It's strange—the ones I waited the longest with were the boyfriends who were my most long-term. It's like the longer we waited, the stronger our relationship became. I realize I probably sound like an After-School Special here, but it's so true. Really think about it before you have sex with him. If he won't be your boyfriend because you won't go all the way, then he doesn't deserve a girlfriend like you anyway!

(And before you do anything sexual, please, please read Chapter 7, "Let's Get Physical"! Promise?)

It's About Time

Okay, you're officially serious. Congrats! I am now going to ask you do to something that will seem very hard at first, but will pay off big in the end. It is the secret to every single successful relationship. And you don't have to buy anything or sign up for anything to get this "secret" formula. It can all be wrapped up in one single sentence. And that sentence is: Do Not See Each Other 24/7! If you're anything like I used to be, you want to see him all the time. And you will not understand why on earth spending as much time with him as humanly possible could be deemed a bad thing. But here's the deal: If you are together every waking moment, you will have nothing to talk about. You will have no lives outside of each other. If you never see your friends, or pursue your interests, or spend time with your family, you just become half of a couple—not a complete unit. And your friends will start to grow resentful. And people will stop inviting you places, because they know you'll say no anyway. And then you and your boyfriend will start to get bored with each other, but you won't know exactly why. Or you'll fight for lack of anything better to do. Or you'll begin to grate on each other's nerves because you're together so much. And if you break up, you're really in trouble because you don't have any friends now. And you can't even remember the kind of things you liked to do because you haven't done them in an eternity. And you have been half of a couple for so long, you no longer feel like a complete person.

Who wants that? I certainly don't. And you shouldn't, either, because you deserve better!

And here's another reason you shouldn't be with him twenty-five hours a day: Things are a lot more interesting when he has a chance to miss you. And how can he miss you when you're with him all the time? Plus, when he goes out with his friends and you go out with yours, you have lots to talk about when you do see each other. The girl he fell for had friends and hobbies and a life. Don't give up all that to keep him, because you will only drive him away. Maintain your own existence! I'm telling you: The best relationships are when two complete people come together. Don't give up who you are just because you have a boyfriend. It's not worth it!

Rings and Things

Sometimes when you're serious, you want to give something to the other person to symbolize how much you care. In our parents' day, it was a class ring, a letter jacket, an ID bracelet. And this is still the case in some parts of the country. But at your school, if a guy gives you his favorite baseball cap, it might mean he's yours forever. Taking this kind of gift from a guy tells him that you're as serious as he is. So don't take something if you're not really into the guy—it will only lead him on, and lead to nothing but trouble. Trust me. And even if you are head over heels, I strongly discourage you from getting his name tattooed on your arm or doing something equally permanent. What happens if you break up next week? Laser tattoo-removal surgery isn't exactly what I'd call fun. And carving your name into your arm, which was all the rage at my junior high for about five minutes, is ill-advised as well. Anything that involves any sort of bleeding or needles is a bad idea. Really bad.

The L-Word

You're boyfriend-girlfriend. You're wearing a necklace he made you from scratch. You are spending lots of quality time with him, but seeing your friends and doing your own thing as well. And you think—no, you know—that you are in love. Deeply. You can't even believe how much you love this guy. He rules! So after you determine that you do indeed love him, the question now becomes "to tell or not to tell." To say it first holds some big risks. If you say it and he doesn't say it back, what happens then? You might feel really rejected, or even question the entire meaning of the relationship. But if he does say it back, you'll feel so great. A definite gamble, and the stakes have never been higher. I rolled the dice with my guy Jay and said, "I love you," about four months into the relationship. Because I did love him, I was certain of it, and couldn't wait another second to tell him. So I did it. Gulp. And then, instead of a verbal response, I got a hug. A hug! I couldn't believe it. When he went to the kitchen a little later, I started crying and called my best friend. I didn't know what to do. She said I should con-front him about it, but I chickened out and just acted like it had never happened. Two weeks later, on our first vacation together, he told me he loved me—and that he'd just been totally taken aback and scared when I said it first. But he loved me 100 percent. It was great! But believe me, those prior two weeks had been pure torture. I was wondering, Does he not feel the same why I do? What's the deal? I was so hurt and con-fused, I really didn't know what to do.

Which brings me to my next point. They always say that if you're going to say "I love you" first, you should just say it because you want to say it and not because you're looking for a response. Sounds good in theory, but in the real world not getting a response feels like a major rejection (or at least it did to me). If you are going to put it out there, you have to prepare yourself for the fact that he might not respond in the way you want him to. You have to be willing to risk what you've got in hopes of kicking things up a notch. He could be too scared to tell you his true feelings and is just waiting for you to say it. Go with your gut here.

But if you want to play it safe and wait for him to say it first, you could be in for some major frustration. You might be bursting to say those three little words while he's not thinking a thing about it. Again, I'm bad at waiting—which is why I got the infamous "hug." You have to weigh the pros and cons and decide for yourself.

Finally, just because someone says he loves you doesn't necessarily mean he does. Love is a verb. It should show in the way he talks to you, treats you, looks at you, kisses you, and acts around you. If he says he loves you but treats you like crap, that's not love. Make sure his actions speak louder than his words!

are you ready to commit?

1. The guy you've been dating wants to go out on Saturday night. You have no other plans. How do you respond?

    a) Say yes in a heartbeat

    b) Say you have to think about it

    c) Say no—you'd rather hang at home instead

2. You've been seeing a guy for a couple of weeks when another guy starts flirting with you at a party. You:

    a) immediately tell him you're dating someone.

    b) chat with him for a few minutes, then say you might see him around.

    c) flirt back, then take his number. What your man doesn't know won't hurt him!

3. You and your mom have just had a major fight. Who do you call?

    a) Your guy, then your best friend

    b) Your best friend, then your guy

    c) Your best friend and that's it

4. Think about the guy you're dating, then fill in the following: He _____ my life.

    a) complements

    b) has little effect on

    c) complicates

5. You're about to go on a date with your guy. How are you feeling?

    a) You can't wait to see him!

    b) You've got definite mixed emotions.

    c) Well, he's better than nobody.

6. It's the end of your date. By now he's totally:

    a) rocking your world.

    b) making you look at your watch.

    c) getting on your nerves.

7. Your guy says he wants to get serious. But you're pretty sure that hot guy in homeroom is going to ask you out. You:

    a) forget Homeroom Man and pledge your love to your fella.

    b) tell him you really need to think about it.

    c) say you'd rather keep it casual for now.

8. You're at a party with your main squeeze. While you're in the kitchen, a gorgeous guy tries to kiss you(!!!). You:

    a) tell him off.

    b) think about it for a second, then push him away.

    c) kiss him back passionately.

9. You see your guy talking to a supermodel look-alike after school. You:

      a) feel a slight twinge of jealousy.

      b) wonder why he's talking to her.

      c) couldn't care less!

10. You've just won two front-row tickets to the year's biggest concert by being the tenth caller. You take:

      a) your guy.

      b) whichever friend wins the coin toss.

      c) your closest girlfriend.

Did you have more A's, B's, or C's? Count them up to find out if you're ready to make it official.

Mostly A's: No Doubt About It!

In your eyes, life would be perfect if you had a boyfriend. Flowers would bloom, birds would sing, and zits would disappear. Heaven! While the right boyfriend can certainly add a lot to your life, he can't make or break it. The quickest route to an awesome existence is having tons of friends, hobbies, and extracurricular activities—and then if you meet the right guy, great. But don't put your life on hold waiting for him to sweep you off your feet. Sweep yourself off your feet first, and fate will take care of the rest.

Mostly B's: Depends on What Day You Ask

Some days the thought of having a boyfriend is super-exciting—a perma-date for every Friday and Saturday, someone you could count on, somebody to love. On other days, the thought of having a boyfriend is about as appealing as having a bad case of poison ivy. You couldn't possibly breathe in a relationship—no way! Being confused about something so major is perfectly natural. Just make sure you think about why it is you're so mixed up on this matter. Are you scared about trusting someone else? Or just not ready for the pressures being in a relationship brings? Pinpoint why you sometimes pull away, then go from there.

Mostly C's: You'd Rather Have a Root Canal

To you, commitment is a four-letter word. You want to do what you want to do when you want to do it without any input from some guy. Sure, guys are fun to hang with—but you're not looking for a boyfriend or anything. It's great to be sensationally single, as long as you're not shutting yourself off from love completely. Are you avoiding commitment because you like the freedom or because you're scared to get hurt? Is it a case of "I'll reject him before he can reject me"? Only you can answer that one, but remember: In the lottery of love, you can't win if you don't enter.

chapter 7

let's get physical

When you're dealing with guys, at some point it's probably going to get physical. Either you're going to kiss him or fool around with him or even go all the way with him. Only you know what you're comfortable with. But I don't have to tell you the risks and dangers out there today. Having unprotected sex with the wrong person can kill you. Period. It's pretty scary stuff. I didn't have sex until I was twenty and was in love. I totally recommend waiting, because it will mean so much more if you actually love the guy and fully know what you're doing. But I know that not everybody operates on the same timetable I did. Some of you might feel ready to have sex at sixteen, while others want to wait until they're married. It's an individual decision. But the main thing to remember is: Do it for yourself, not for the guy. I didn't even have an orgasm with the first two guys I was with—and one guy I dated for over a year! So why did I even bother having sex with them? I wasn't getting pleasure—they were. But that was the whole point. I wanted to please them. Now I realize that good sex is all about pleasing both of you. It's not fair if he gets off and you're just sitting there feeling frustrated and left out. And if you "fake it," you are cheating both of you! The right partner will care about your needs as well as his own, no matter if you're just making out or actually having sex. Consider this chapter sort of a crash course on all things sexual. And remember—just because you read about it doesn't mean you have to do it. Or that I even recommend you do it. But if you do decide you want to take things a step further, at least you'll know what the risks are. You can never know too much about your body, so study up.

The Kiss

You've gone on a really great date. Are you obligated to give him a good-night kiss? No. Even if you really like the guy, you don't have to do anything you don't feel comfortable doing. I once went out with a guy five times before I even kissed him. There is no time limit. Hey, you might even feel like you want to smooch him five minutes into the date. Just follow your heart.

Making Out

Okay, you're kissing. Then you kiss some more. Then he's sticking his tongue in your mouth. You do this for a while. Then you come up for air. Guess what? You're making out. But, again, don't do anything you don't want to do. If he's making you feel uncomfortable, pull away. If things are moving too quickly, tell him you want to slow down. You're in control. Don't let him just do whatever he wants to you. He'll respect you more in the long run for having your own brain and your own boundaries.

Fooling Around

Taking making out a step further is what most call fooling around. You're French-kissing, he's feeling up your chest, or maybe you're even rubbing each other's privates. You're not having sex, but you're definitely doing something sexual. Remember, do not travel beyond your comfort zone. If you have a strange feeling about something, stop doing it. You are under no obligations. Fooling around can be fun if you're into it. But if you're not, you'll just feel pressured and freaked out. And what's the fun in that?

Hands On

If you touch the guy's penis until he has an orgasm, this is called giving a hand job. You can't get pregnant from giving one, but it can be hard to figure out exactly how to do it at first. Guys usually like it better when you use some sort of lubrication, like K-Y jelly, Vaseline, or even spit. Have him touch himself first so you know exactly how he likes it. It can feel weird at first, but you'll get better with practice. Again, don't do it unless you want to!

If a guy rubs your clitoris, you're receiving the female version of a hand job. You can't get pregnant from this, either, but guys usually don't know how to do it unless you teach them. Show him how you like to be touched, or give him instructions while he's rubbing you. Some girls like this and some girls don't. Only do what feels comfortable to you.

Oral Report

Oral sex (or "going down" on somebody) is when you use your mouth and tongue to stimulate someone sexually, usually by kissing and sucking his or her genitals. Like everything else, some people are into it and some aren't. The main worry here among most girls is smelling bad, but if you take regular showers, believe me, you're fine. Don't panic. Giving (and receiving) oral sex takes some practice since it feels a bit strange at first.

The good thing about oral sex is that you can turn each other on without fear of pregnancy. But just like with intercourse, you need to use a condom or dental dam because many diseases (including HIV) can be transmitted orally.

If a guy ejaculates while you're giving him a blow job, his semen will end up in your mouth unless he's wearing a condom (which he should be) or if he "pulls out." But since some semen (pre-cum) escapes before ejaculation, disease can be transmitted that way, too. That's why condoms are a necessity.

Like I said, receiving oral sex can feel weird at first. In fact, I used to pretty much hate it! But since your clitoris is the most sensitive part of your body, cunnilingus (as it is technically known) is what many girls like best. Just relax and don't put any pressure on yourself to feel a certain way. Enjoy. And if you don't like it, that's okay, too. There is no right or wrong way to feel during any sexual act. Every person responds differently.

Let's Talk About Sex, Baby

If you decide to "go all the way," protect yourself. Use a condom. I know many guys will resist (because I've dated a few opposers myself), but you'll be surprised how quickly they'll comply once they figure out that unless they wear one they aren't getting any. Short of abstinence, a condom is the most effective way to protect yourself against sexually transmitted diseases (STDs) and HIV. And it is effective against pregnancy, too. Speaking of, birth control is a must. Why? Because you don't want to have a baby while you're still so young, that's why.

 You might have this glamorized notion that having a baby will really bond you with the father. Wrong! Many guys take off once they find out a girl is pregnant. It's not right, but it's reality. And do you really want to bring a life into the world when your own life is really just beginning? Having a baby will rob you of so many opportunities and experiences. Do yourself a favor and protect yourself—and your future. Use birth control!

That said, the decision to have sex or not is a monumental one. Don't be pressured into it. First of all, having intercourse means risking pregnancy. And, as a girl, you're the one who would ultimately have to deal with those consequences. It's not fair, I know, but it's true. You've got to use protection. And no birth control except for abstinence is 100 percent effective. Plus you've got to think about the risk of sexually transmitted diseases. There are about a million of them out there! And some of them can kill you. On an emotional level, having sex means you are going to feel all sorts of new feelings—both good and bad. The highs will be higher, but the lows will be lower. And there's this whole other factor introduced into your relationship. Deciding to have sex isn't a

BE IN CONTROL

If you're going to have sex, you owe it to yourself to use birth control and protection. It takes seconds, and can change (or even save) your whole life! Here are your choices:

♥ CONDOMS WITH FOAM—excellent against STDs and pregnancy

♥ CONDOMS—excellent against STDs; good against pregnancy

♥ FOAM—fair against STDs; good against pregnancy

♥ DIAPHRAGM—poor against STDs; excellent against pregnancy

♥ CERVICAL CAP—poor against STDs; good against pregnancy

♥ THE PILL—no protection against STDs; excellent against pregnancy

♥ DEPO-PROVERA—no protection against STDs; excellent against pregnancy

♥ NORPLANT—no protection against STDs; excellent against pregnancy

♥ IUD—no protection against STDs; excellent against pregnancy

♥ WITHDRAWAL—no protection against STDs; poor against pregnancy

one-time decision. Once you have it, it will become an issue from that point forward.

Not to say that sex can't be a totally wonderful thing in a committed relationship. It can. But just make sure you're ready and you're doing it for the right reasons. Only you can know if you're ready or not. But don't jump into it without thinking about it heavily. It's a major decision.

And if you're thinking about having casual sex, please think again. It's a really bad idea and it's life-threatening. How many people has this guy been with? Has he ever used IV drugs? If you don't know him that well, you can't possibly know the answers to these questions. And if you feel like the guy doesn't "look" like he has a disease, I've got news for you: You can't tell if someone has an STD just by looking at him. I knew a guy in high school who had HIV who was totally normal-looking and popular and gorgeous. But he died soon after his twenty-first birthday. It's really scary. This is something our parents never had to deal with. They had to think about pregnancy, for sure, but we have to think about dying. Don't risk your life for

THE BIG LIE

You know how some guys tell you that you can't get pregnant during your period? Well, you can! You've got to use protection, even if you're getting your monthly visit from Aunt Flo! Use it every time.

sex. It's not worth it! And if you think it couldn't happen to you, do you think anybody ever thinks it could happen to them? The terrifying thing is that it could happen to any one of us.

If you do want to hook up with a guy you don't really know, be safe about it. Try mutual masturbation or just messing around. To put it bluntly, you can still have an orgasm without having sex. And if you do decide to have intercourse, you are putting yourself at a million times more risk. Is it really worth it?

The Big "O"

In the movies, everyone reaches orgasm every time. Bells whistle, sirens blow, and fireworks go off. In the real world, it can be a little more tricky. A lot of girls don't have orgasms—especially when they first start having sex. Why? Because most girls need to have stimulation until their whole pelvic area feels aroused. Many guys just stick it in and they're done. And something that's even more disheartening is that a lot of girls feel like they have to "fake it" so the guy won't feel like a failure. I did this continuously with my first boyfriend. I didn't want him to feel like he wasn't good enough, so I just moaned until he thought that I had climaxed. But I now know that faking it doesn't make sex better—it makes it worse. If the sex isn't good for you, you have to tell your partner you're not having an orgasm and try to find ways to improve the situation together. Maybe you need to try other positions or spend more time in foreplay. The point is, you both should get to have orgasms—not just him. And if he thinks you're having one when you're really not, you can't blame him entirely for not delivering. How can he fix the problem if he doesn't even know there is one? It's all about honesty. When you're honest with your boyfriend in the bedroom, things will totally fall into place.

Disease Data

There are scads of STDs out there besides HIV/AIDS: Herpes, gonorrhea, crabs, genital warts, hepatitis, chlamydia, syphilis, vaginal infections, and scabies, to name just a few. They're not all life-threatening, but not one of them is fun to have. The best way to protect yourself (besides abstinence) is to use a condom. If you think you have an STD or want more information, call the STD Hotline at 1-800-227-8922. The HIV/AIDS Hotline is 1-800-342-AIDS. Remember: The only stupid question is the one you don't ask.

Peer Pressure

If he's trying to get you into bed, he might try a number of tactics. He may say if you loved him, you'd do it. Well, if he loved *you*, he'd respect your opinion! It's a two-way street. You can't let someone guilt you into this big of a decision. Maybe he says he's in physical pain because you won't do it with him, which some guys refer to as "blue balls." No one has ever died of this, trust me! Just tell him if he's in that much pain, he should go ahead and masturbate. That should shut him up. The only reason you should ever have sex with someone is because you have fully thought about it and decided it's the right decision for you—not him! Don't fall for his head games and guilt trips. Hang tough!

The Price of Partying

If you're drinking or using drugs, your judgment is going to be altered. You're not going to make the kinds of logical, clear-headed decisions that you'd make when you're sober. So if you're around someone you don't really know that well or on a first date, don't let drugs or alcohol make your decisions for you! They will only lower your defenses and make you more likely to put yourself in a compromising position. Some people do drugs or drink so they will act differently than they normally would and feel less uptight. But when you're intoxicated or high, you'll be less likely to use protection—and, as I've said, that could end up killing you. Talk about a buzz kill.

Being Raped

If you're forced to have sex against your will, that's rape. Maybe you've just gone on a date with someone and he forces himself on you. Or maybe a stranger drags you into a back alley and takes you sexually. They're both rape—and are both against the law. (For prevention info, go to pages 99–101) As I said in Chapter 5, I hope you are never raped. But if you are, it is not your fault—no matter how much you've had to drink or have already done with the guy. No means no. If you've been raped, you need to get help immediately. Get yourself to a safe place with someone you trust. Call your local rape-crisis hotline immediately. They'll send someone to accompany you to the police station and/or emergency room. Someone who's been through

this before will come to your side and be on your team. Rape is a terrifying experience, and you don't need to suffer alone. Report what happened to you, even if you're embarrassed. Let your voice be heard.

The Bottom Line

Since there's so much ground to cover when it comes to sex, I realize I've barely scratched the surface here. I mean, sex is a whole book in itself. And there are tons of great books out there, filled with things you should know before going all the way. I challenge you to learn as much as you can on the subject before making the decision to have or not have sex. That way you'll know that you've made the best, most educated decision possible, no matter what you decide. I really hope you'll do what's right for you, and not what's right for someone else. Because you're awesome, and you owe it to yourself to stay true to your convictions and to protect your life and your future.

Quiz

are you ready for sex?

1. In your opinion, could you pass a Sex Ed course right this second?
- a) Without a doubt
- b) Maybe, maybe not
- c) No way

2. Would you know how to put a condom on a guy?
- a) Yes
- b) Not sure
- c) No

3. How many times have you discussed sex with your partner?
- a) Six or more (times?)
- b) Three to five
- c) Two or less

4. Why do you want to have sex?
- a) Because you are emotionally ready
- b) To show how grown-up you are
- c) To make your boyfriend love you more

5. If your relationship was in trouble, do you think sex could make it better?

      a) You don't think it would matter either way.

      b) It all depends on the relationship.

      c) Yes, totally

6. How many times has your boyfriend tried to pressure you into sex?

      a) Never

      b) A few times

      c) Many times

7. If you did have sex, do you think you'd feel guilty or upset afterward?

      a) No

      b) Probably

      c) For sure

8. Are you planning to have sex on a specific day, like after the prom or on your anniversary?

      a) No, why would I?

      b) That wouldn't be a bad idea.

      c) Of course

9. Do you trust and respect your potential partner?

      a) Immensely

      b) Somewhat

      c) Not really

10. Would you feel comfortable purchasing condoms?
    a) Sure
    b) I don't know.
    c) No

11. Do you plan on using birth control?
    a) Absolutely
    b) Unsure
    c) No

12. If "pulling out" was the method of birth control your partner insisted upon, would you refuse to have sex?
    a) Yes
    b) Maybe
    c) No

13. Do you plan on using a condom every time?
    a) Yes
    b) I don't know.
    c) No

14. Will you more than likely get drunk or use drugs before having sex?
    a) No
    b) I might.
    c) Yes

Mostly A's: Incredibly in-the-Know

Your responses indicate that you've really done your homework. You've educated yourself about STDs, know the consequences of unprotected sex, and fully trust your partner. Congratulations for being so sex-savvy. Just think it over long and hard before you decide one way or the other. It's a very big deal.

Mostly B's: Somewhat Savvy

You know some stuff about certain aspects of sex, but are totally clueless about others. You need to know all there is to know about sex before you decide whether to have it. The fact is, you can't afford to not be 100 percent clear about stuff like condoms or birth control. Get smart, then make your decision.

Mostly C's: Completely Clueless

You're simply not ready to have sex yet. Why? You don't know much about it, for one thing. You wouldn't just jump behind the wheel a car without taking Driver's Ed, would you? The same is true about sex. You've got to learn all you can. Because doing it before you're ready will only end up hurting you in the end.

chapter 8

reach out and touch someone

What's the most important aspect of a great relationship? No, it's not the dating. And it's not even the kissing (even though that's incredibly important!). The most important aspect of a relationship is actually communication. If you can't communicate with your partner, you're done. Over. Finished. Because the way you express your thoughts and feelings will ultimately make or break your relationship. Now, in an ideal world, there would be a class on this—like "How to Talk to Your Boyfriend 101" or something. But unfortunately no such class exists.

Therefore, I've decided to develop a crash course of my own. In the next few pages, you'll learn how to tell him you're pissed without starting World War III, how to let him know exactly what you're thinking, and how to become a better listener. You'll be tested on all this after you're done—so take lots of notes! (Just kidding about the test part, but there will be a quiz to determine your communicating rating.) So sharpen those pencils, and listen up . . .

Communication Nation

You might think it's ludicrous to have to learn how to talk to someone. I mean, you've known how to talk since you were two, right? But the thing is, even though you know how to talk, that doesn't necessarily mean you know how to communicate effectively. Because it's tough. With my first couple of boyfriends, I was a total lunatic. When I'd get mad, I would never say so—I'd just act like everything was fine until my anger would build up and build up and eventually explode. Obviously that wasn't exactly healthy communication, but that's the way I had somehow learned to express myself. Maybe you've seen your parents act a certain way, so that's how you act. Or your friends do it, so you simply follow suit. We all learn by example, but that doesn't necessarily mean those examples are good ones. It's hard to change your behavior, it really is. It took a long time for me to be able to tell my boyfriends that I was mad about something. I was scared they'd break up with me or hate me for it. But in reality being honest with my boyfriends only strengthened my relationships. It was much more damaging to act happy when I wasn't.

Let's say you get mad about something. He says something to hurt your feelings, for example. How do you react? The best way to handle the situation is to tell him that what he said really hurt your feelings. Oftentimes, though, girls will either (a) not say anything and act like everything is cool (like I used to), (b) start screaming at him, putting him on the defensive and causing a major battle, (c) give him the silent treatment but not tell him why they're mad, or (d) silently decide to "punish" him by not making out with him that night or not helping him work on his term paper like they'd promised. Now, in each of these four examples, there's one major problem: He doesn't know how you feel, and the issue never gets truly resolved. You've got to come clean. Because having a relationship is all about relating. If you can't relate, you're dead in the water. But it's hard at first and definitely takes some practice. You will probably feel ridiculous doing this (I know I did), but it works. Ask your best friend to come over, and

tell her you want to practice talking to your boyfriend with her. Create a likely scenario, such as him arriving a half hour late for a date. Then role-play how you would handle it. Tell "him" you're really upset about his tardiness, because your time is valuable and you don't deserve to be kept waiting. Tell "him" you've been sitting there for the last thirty minutes worrying that he was in a car wreck, and that you don't think it's fair he put you through that. Tell "him" everything you want to say. And then have your best friend react in the way she thinks he would. Have her agree with you, apologize, or blow up. Then continue the game. The more comfortable you feel in these fake situations, the more comfortable you'll feel during the real ones.

Even if you're a good communicator, however, that doesn't necessarily mean your boyfriend is. If he's got some problems with communication, you've got to discuss them with him. Don't attack or criticize, or he might not listen. Talk to him when things are going right, not in the middle of the fight. A good opening line might be: "Hey, I've noticed that when we disagree about something, we have a lot of problems communicating. I tend to _____, and you tend to _____. I really think our relationship would be a lot better if we could work on that. What do you think?" (Put this in your own words so you don't sound like a self-help book.) At this point, he'll likely agree—because who doesn't want a better relationship? Then you can brainstorm some ideas for more effective communicating. Here are a few to get you started:

• Design a code word to use when things start getting out of hand. If he starts raising his voice or you feel like you're about to lose it, one of you could say "kiwi" or whatever word you've chosen. This would let the other one know a time-out is in order. You could both count to twenty or immediately listen to a favorite song when the code word is mentioned; anything to break the tension.

• Mirroring is an oldie but a goodie. When you tell him that you're upset about something, he has to repeat what you've said in his own words. For example, when you say, "I'm pissed you blew me off on Friday night. It made me feel really abandoned and upset. It ruined my whole evening," He'll then say, "I understand that you're pissed that I blew you off on Friday night. I realize I made you feel really abandoned and upset. By going out with my friends without even calling you, I ruined your whole evening." This ensures that he's actually listening to what you say. You do the same when he says something to you. It sounds a little hokey, but it actually works.

• Make a pact to be honest with each other. If you're upset about something, agree to discuss it rather than just brushing it under the rug. Sign a certificate stating your promise, then keep your word.

- Vow to never raise your voice or name-call during fights.

- Create coupons for each other to give during arguments. One he gives you might say, "I screwed up—Good for one free chick-flick viewing, without me griping or complaining about it." This will inject some humor into your battles and can really lighten things up.

Telling each other when someone does something right is another great communication tool. If he left you a note on your car and it really made your day, tell him so. People need positive reinforcement. It's sometimes easier to dwell on the bad things than the good. Let him know what exactly you appreciate about him, and make sure he does the same.

But when you're trying to overhaul your communication skills, be prepared: You can't change overnight, and it's something that you really have to work on consistently to make a difference. But it is so worth it. Your relationships will be stronger, you'll feel better about yourself, and you'll have so much less stress. It's totally worth the effort!

Passing Notes

Writing little notes to each other is one more great way to communicate with your man. But if you're writing the notes at school, never put something in writing that you wouldn't want the whole school to hear. Why not? Let my own degrading example illustrate. It's the first day of school, ninth grade. I'm sitting in Earth Science next to Mike, the guy I like. I write him a note asking him if he has a girlfriend. I pass it to him. The teacher, Mr. Horn, sees me do it. He confiscates the note and then proceeds to READ IT ALOUD to the entire class. It was the most humiliating moment of my life! I could barely show my face in that class after that, and I begged my parents to  let me transfer. Please spare yourself the embarrassment. Don't put anything—and I do mean anything—in writing that you wouldn't want the whole world to know. But if you must, at least develop a secret code that would be tough to crack. If you don't, you're risking total mortification. Trust me!

That said, notes are a great place to broach topics you might be too embarrassed to bring up face-to-face. And leaving him a little note that lets him know how much you care can mean so much. If you want to get more creative, leave him an audio love letter in his car's cassette player with a note telling him to hit "play." I did this for Jay, and he loved it!

The Final Word

Communicating with your boyfriend involves a lot more than picking up the phone and dialing his digits. It takes courage to share your wants and needs, especially since sometimes it seems easier just to keep quiet about whatever's bugging you. But you're doing you both a big favor by speaking out. Because the more you communicate, the better your relationship will be. Be brave. Tell him what's on your mind, and encourage him to do the same. Your relationship will be the better for it.

Quiz what's your communicating rating?

1. When you're mad at your guy, you:
    a) give him the silent treatment.
    b) totally freak out on him—yelling and screaming your lungs out.
    c) try to discuss it rationally.

2. When you want to ask a guy out, you:
    a) beg a friend to ask him out for you.
    b) convince yourself he'll say no, then chicken out.
    c) go up to him and see if he wants to hang out.

3. A guy gives you his number and tells you to call him. You:

   a) call him.

   b) call him, then hang the phone up when someone answers.

   c) never call.

4. You met an awesome guy on-line and he's just written you the nicest e-mail ever. You:

   a) wait two days to e-him back (to avoid looking too anxious).

   b) e-mail him back immediately.

   c) forward it to all of your friends before responding.

5. Your boyfriend just got a new beeper. When he goes out with his buds, how many times do you page him?

   a) One or less

   b) Two to four

   c) More than five

6. You're writing your boyfriend a juicy note. How do you sign it?

   a) "Love" (it's true, after all)

   b) "Love ya" (way less serious than love)

   c) "See ya" (keep him guessing)

7. Your boyfriend wants to eat Chinese, but you're in the mood for pizza. How do you resolve it?

   a) Go for stir-fry without saying anything.

   b) Agree to have pizza for dinner and fortune cookies for dessert.

   c) Have such a big fight that the date ends before dinner even starts.

8. You're calling him for the first time and the answering machine picks up. Now what?

    a) You say whatever's on the top of your head.

    b) Hang up, write out what you're going to say, then call back and recite it.

    c) Slam the phone down without leaving a message and hope he doesn't have Caller ID.

Scoring:

1. a) 2; b) 1; c) 3   **5.** a) 3; b) 2; c) 1

2. a) 2; b) 1; c) 3   **6.** a) 3; b) 2; c) 1

3. a) 3; b) 2; c) 1   **7.** a) 2; b) 3; c) 1

4. a) 2; b) 3; c) 1   **8.** a) 2; b) 3; c) 1

Add up your score to find out how well you get your point across.

17–24: Communication Queen

When you're mad, your guy knows it. And when you're happy, he knows it, too. You believe that it's not even worth having a relationship if you can't tell your boyfriend how you feel. As long as you don't spill all of your secrets on the first date (boundaries, baby, boundaries), you're set.

12–16: Communication Gap

Sometimes you're great about communicating with your man— stating your mind, standing up for your beliefs, keeping your cool. At others, you have a harder time letting him know how you feel. Learning how to get your point across effectively takes some work, but it pays off in spades. Remember: Practice makes perfect!

7–11: Miss Miscommunication

Ever wanted to tell your guy something really important, but then you totally blew up at him during your intro and he tuned the rest of your story out? Or have you ever felt too nervous to talk to him before even uttering a syllable? Your lines of communication are completely clogged. If you want to save your relationship, work on this problem today. Don't wait.

chapter 9

unconventional love

Boy meets girl, boy falls in love with girl, boy and girl live happily ever after. That's the equation, right? I don't think so! Now that the 1900s are behind us, the equations for love are a lot more complicated. Like boy meets girl, boy falls in love with girl, then boy moves fifteen hundred miles away. Or boy e-mails girl, girl e-mails back, and girl falls madly in love with boy even though she's never met him face-to-face. Thoroughly confused yet? Don't worry—a lot of your perplexity is about to be cleared up in the next couple of pages. You'll learn how to make a long-distance love last, what you should do before meeting your cyber-Romeo, whether or not a summer fling equals cheating . . . and more.

Long-Distance Love

You're madly in love with a boy, and he tells you he's going to school in Alaska. Or you meet the guy of your dreams, only to find out he's visiting from England. However you get involved in a long-distance relationship, one thing is for sure: They're not easy. It is possible to make one last, but it takes a lot of work. Because when your boy is thousands of miles away, he's not really part of your day-to-day life. Sure, you might call, write, or e-mail, but he's not someone you can just hang out with during an afternoon or go see the latest slasher flick with on a Saturday night. The upside to all this is that you will get these fabulous letters and cards from the man of your dreams, and you will get to compose equally creative missives for him. Plus, if he's extra inventive, he'll make you mix-tapes and collages and all sorts of wonderful stuff. Heading to your mailbox has never been so much fun!

But sometimes letters or e-mails simply can't cut it. And this is where the phone comes in. First of all, your bills will be through the roof—making you work extra-long hours at your after-school job or causing major battles between yourself and your parents. And your phone calls will start becoming as important as dates, since they're the closest thing you've got. If he says one thing to make you mad (or you him), a major fight can easily ensue. And if you call him and he's not home, you might wonder who he's out with and whether she's cuter than you are. And he'll be thinking the same thing when he can't reach you. It's gut-wrenching.

The biggest upside to long-distance love is the visits. Suddenly, when you're together, the whole world seems to make sense. You're in the same town—finally! But a lot of pressure comes along with that. You're only seeing each other for a short amount of time, so you're trying to cram in months of fun and dates and kisses and conversations into a few days. Tempers are bound to flare when you're so pressured to have a perfect time. It's important to set realistic expectations. You want to have fun, sure, but you don't want to set your sights so high that nothing can measure up. Just relax and focus on being together. Because that's what it's all about.

If you or your boyfriend decide to go to a college far away, you've got a big decision to make. Should you try to make it work long-distance or just go your separate ways? What your answer should be depends completely on your relationship. How long have you been together? How serious are you? How often would you get to see each other? Remember that a long-distance relationship takes a lot of nurturing. And, when you're in one, you're shutting your-self off from all the potential dates you'll meet at college. Are you willing to do that?

THINGS YOU CAN DO FOR YOUR LONG-DISTANCE LOVE

♥ Mail him a box of homemade chocolate cookies.

♥ Send him a balloon bouquet on his birthday.

♥ Make a tape of yourself talking (à la Felicity) and mail it to him.

♥ Start a joint journal: You write a couple of entries, then send it to him and encourage him to do the same. Keep sending it back and forth until it's full!

♥ Borrow Dad's video camera and make him a documentary about your life. Take it to friends' houses, school, parties—everywhere you go, it goes!

♥ Create a scrapbook of all the times you've spent together.

♥ Send him a postcard every single day for a month just for fun.

♥ On Valentine's Day, send him a big box of blank cards and lots of stamps—so he has no excuse not to write!

♥ Leave him silly messages on his answering machine.

♥ Send him a care package full of candy, dime-store toys, and personalized love notes.

Really mull it over before you make your decision. If you're unde-
cided, you can always agree to try it for a month and then go
from there.

If you decide to stick it out, there are a few things you've got
to do. First, you've got to stay social. Even though your boyfriend
isn't around, you must make yourself go out with your friends
and stay busy. Otherwise, you'll resent your boyfriend for holding
you back. And you have to trust each other. If you don't trust
him, you can't be in a successful long-distance relationship with
him, because there's no possible way for you to keep tabs on his
actions. Make a pact that if one of you is tempted to cheat, you'll
break it off. You owe each other that much. And, thirdly, you
must make a concentrated effort to stay connected through calls
and letters. Let him know what's going on in your life. Share your
thoughts and fears, and make sure he does the same. If you
don't know what's going on in the other one's head, you can't
have a relationship. It's that simple.

But be prepared for the down times, because there are going
to be many. When all your friends are going out with their
boyfriends, you'll feel cheated that you can't go out with yours.
You'll start to feel lonely between visits, missing his hugs and
kisses. And if another guy starts to show interest, it's hard not to
be tempted—even after you made that stay-true pact with your
man. After all, the guy hitting on you is someone you could go to
the park with on a Sunday afternoon or hang out with after class,
and your boyfriend isn't.

Making long-distance love work is difficult, but not impossible. If you're with the right guy and are willing to make the sacrifices, your romance will survive. But it's not easy. And only you can decide whether or not it's worth it.

Cyber Love

If you spend a lot of time on-line, you've probably met plenty of people in chat rooms or through bulletin boards—people you may even consider close friends, though you've never met face-to-face. And sometimes that friendship turns into something more. You exchange photos, start e-mailing each other every day, maybe even talk on the phone—and all of a sudden you notice something odd. You sort of . . . like this person. As in, *like* like. And it turns out your crush feels the same way. You decide to take your friendship to the next level. Congratulations! You are now in a relationship with someone you've never even seen in real life!

CYBER PROTECTION

Cyberspace can be a dangerous place, indeed. Here's how you can protect yourself on-line.

• **Keep personal facts to yourself.**
Don't reveal your address, phone number, favorite hangouts, or where you go to school. This info can be used against you if it lands in the wrong hands.

• Don't believe everything you hear.

It's easy to make up stuff in cyberspace. Fifty-year-old men might say they're fifteen and gorgeous; guys might say they're girls wanting to get together for a sleepover. It's fine to chat with someone on-line and have a good time—as long as you remember things aren't always what they appear. There's a chance your cyber-sweetie could turn out to be a serious sociopath, so you have to be careful.

• Never meet someone by yourself off-line.

Even though you may think it'd be exciting to meet your on-line love for a secret date, it's extremely dangerous. If you do decide to meet face to face, do so in a well-populated public place, such as a mall or skating rink, and bring along rein-forcements—your friends, your siblings, even your parents. Some girls who haven't followed these guidelines have been kidnapped or raped, so don't take the risk.

• Ignore cybersleaze.

Don't dignify obscene e-mail or nasty chat-room chatter with a response. Instead, jet a copy of all offensive messages over to your system operator, who will kick the offender off-line once and for all.

   If an on-line ex won't leave you alone, change your e-mail address. It's a pain, but it's worth getting away from someone who won't get the hint.

Even though it sounds kind of strange, it does happen—a lot. With millions of teenagers on-line, it's bound to. And sometimes it actually works out. You know why? Because an on-line relationship is all about getting to know the person on the inside and finding out what they're really like instead of just focusing on appearance and things like that. You're friends first, so your romance has a stable foundation.

But on-line relationships do have their share of problems. For starters, the person you think you're falling for may not even exist. See, on-line, people can easily take on different personae. Just because your crush claims to be a normal, attractive seventeen-year-old who loves baseball and Korn doesn't mean anything; he could actually be a forty-seven-year-old ex-con for all you know. Anyone could make up a fake name, fake age, and fake interests, and even send you a fake picture. So use caution. If you think you might be interested in someone on-line, go very slowly. Until you know him well enough to feel confident he's legit, keep your phone number and your home address to yourself. Ask lots and lots of questions, and keep track of his answers by saving the e-mails he sends you. That way if some-

ARE YOU READY FOR CYBERSEX?

Just like the real thing (see Chapter 7, page 129), you shouldn't do it unless you're ready. And you may never be ready—that's perfectly okay. Just don't let a guy pressure you into it. Because it will only make you feel sleazy unless you're into it, too!

thing doesn't match up, you'll know you're not just remember-ing wrong. And if he says anything inconsistent or suspicious, break off contact immediately.

An on-line relationship means spending a lot of time—you guessed it—on-line. Beware: Your parents may start complaining that you're wasting hours a day on the computer, or even ground you from using it. Although you may not see the time as wasted, they may have a point. Do you really want to be glued to your computer when you could be hanging with friends, kick-boxing, or just curled up with a good book? At this point in your life, are you prepared to sacrifice the relation-ship benefits that come packaged with proximity? Ask yourself if an on-line relation-ship is really the best thing for you right now. If you think it is, keep your life in balance. See your friends, and maintain your interests. And instead of always relying on e-mail, send letters now and then, or exchange cassette tapes so you can hear each other's voices.

Okay, say you do build trust over time, and you find yourself falling for each other. You decide you want to—gasp!—meet face-to-face. Before you actually do, tell people about it. Don't be secretive, because the more people who know about it, the safer you'll be. And consider bringing along a friend to the meeting. There's safety in numbers. Sorry if I sound paranoid here, but there are a lot of crazy people lurking on the Internet. Hopefully your cyber-boyfriend isn't one of them, but he very well could be. It's better to be safe than sorry. And it is imperative that you meet in a public place. Meeting him at a hotel or at some unknown address is asking for trouble. (See "Cyber Protection," page 164, for more details.) You've got to take care of yourself. And if he's an upstanding guy, he'll understand that.

When you do meet him, it's probably going to be awkward, so go easy on yourselves. Talk about the fact that it's going to be stressful before you meet. Bringing a friend along could really break the ice. Plan to go out to eat or do something active (like bowling). That way, you'll have something to do besides just stare at each other and feel freaked. And hopefully you'll like each other as much in person as you did on-line. But if you

WHERE THE BOYS ARE

On vacation? Here's where to do some prime boy-watching.

Hotel pool or hot tub
Beach
Arcade
Water park
Mall
Sporting arena
Amusement park
Comic-book store
All-ages club
Concert

don't, at least you gave it a shot. If you learned something in the process, you didn't really lose at all.

Seasonal Sizzle

Maybe you're on spring break when you suddenly spot the cutest guy you've ever seen in your life. You plot to make him yours—if only for one week! Or perhaps you're on the beach when you totally fall for that luscious lifeguard looming over the ocean. So what if it's just a summer romance? You'd take some mouth-to-mouth from him anytime! Seasonal love—like summer romances or spring flings—can be a lot of fun. They can add drama to your vacation, making it seem more like a soap opera than your actual life. And they'll provide lots to tell your friends back home about. The downside? They aren't always as serious as maybe you'd want them to be. And if the guy is from another part of the country, you may never see him again. But sometimes that's the chance you've got to take!

If you have a boyfriend back home, you might wonder if you should feel guilty about your vacation rendezvous. If you'll never see the guy again and your boyfriend will never find out, is it still cheating? If you're serious about your man, I think so. But if you and your guy are not exclusive, then there's no harm seeing another guy—as long as you're safe about it. Some couples even agree to take spring break or summers "off" to alleviate any guilt. I am too much of a one-man woman to buy into this kind of arrangement, but if it works for you, go for it.

If you find yourself falling in love with your holiday hunk, take a step back. Unless you both agree you like each other enough to try and make it work long-distance, you should attempt to see the situation for what it is: a fun diversion. Since spring breaks and summer vacations are all about escaping from reality, faraway flings fit into this category as well. Half the fun of meeting someone on vacation is the fact that you're totally out of your element and so far removed from the real world. You can be whoever you want to be. If you're a bookish loner back home, you can be a vivacious beach bunny on vacation and the guys will be none the wiser. It's like taking a break from your life. And that's why most summer romances don't turn into anything more: because they're not rooted in reality. And that's okay!

When it's time to say good-bye to your man, try not to be too depressed. After all, you'll always have the memories of your time together. Take pictures of him so you can always remember his piercing eyes or gorgeous smile. And go ahead and exchange e-mail addresses or phone numbers if you want to keep in touch. Who knows? You might just meet up again someday.

Quiz: what are your together-forever odds?

1. How often do you talk to each other?

a) Once a day or more

b) Every few days

c) Once a week or less

2. In one of your letters, you mention a new guy at school. How does he react?

a) Asks you if you think the guy is cute

b) Acts a little jealous but keeps it under control

c) Proceeds to tell you about the hot new chick in his Chem class

3. How far apart do you live?

a) Five hundred miles or less

b) Five hundred to one thousand miles

c) Over one thousand miles

4. Have you agreed to see other people?

a) Of course

b) Not exactly, but what he doesn't know won't hurt him.

c) No way

5. If you haven't met your guy face-to-face, do you plan to?

(If you have, give yourself 1 point.)

a) I don't know

b) Doubt it

c) Yes

6. If you're in a fight with your faraway love, how do you handle it?

a) Give him the silent treatment for a few days

b) Call and work it out

c) Go out with someone else

7. How often do you visit each other?

a) Never

b) At least once a month

c) Once every few months

8. If you're going out with your friends, what does your guy do?

a) Makes you call him every hour

b) Gets totally pissed off

c) Goes out with his friends

Will it last? Add up your score to find out.

Scoring:

1. a) 1; b) 2; c) 3
2. a) 2; b) 1; c) 3
3. a) 1; b) 2; c) 3
4. a) 1; b) 3; c) 2

5. a) 2; b) 3; c) 1
6. a) 2; b) 1; c) 3
7. a) 3; b) 1; c) 2
8. a) 3; b) 2; c) 1

8–13: Happily Ever After

Long-term love is definitely in the air! Don't get me wrong—you and your man definitely have your problems. But the fact that you're willing to face them head-on puts you shoulders above the rest. If you continue to cut each other slack and work things out, you'll have a long, beautiful relationship.

14–19: Fixer-Upper

Your unconventional love does have its good points, but it needs some work if it's going to make it in the long haul. Love is hard enough, even when you're not hundreds (or thousands) of miles away from each other. You both need to be aware of the challenges you'll face and vow to hurdle them together. Love conquers all!

20–24: Snowball's Chance in Hell

Unless you two do a total 180, this is not going to work. Your biggest problem? You don't communicate. And when you're in a hands-off relationship like yours, communicating is basically all you've got. Without it, you're done. So either make the break now or give your relationship the makeover it so desperately needs. Good luck with whatever you decide (because you're going to need it).

making the break

So you and your man are still together. Only things aren't going so great. Maybe you like someone else. Or maybe he's just getting on your nerves. At any rate, you want out. But how are you going to do it? Breaking up with a guy can be a harrowing experience. (As can being broken up with, but that's covered in the next chapter.) You don't want to hurt the guy's feelings, but you have a sneaking suspicion you're going to have to if you want out of this relationship. Never fear. In these pages, you will find out how to break up with him without breaking his heart, discover whether or not it's possible to stay friends, and learn what you should do if he—gulp—starts crying or something. Happy hightailing!

Should You Do It?

Deciding whether or not to make the break isn't easy. If you've only been dating two weeks and just found out he cheated on you, it's a no-brainer. He's gone. But if you've been dating for six months and have slowly come to the realization that you like him more as a friend than a boyfriend, it's a bit trickier.

When you're deciding whether or not to make the break, you have to ask yourself one simple question: "Would my life be better without him?" Really think about it. Would you have more fun if he wasn't in the picture? Does the thought of dating other guys excite you? If so, you're definitely heading toward a split. But if you feel more sad than glad about life without him, maybe you should talk to him about what you'd like to change in the relationship. Perhaps you're in a rut and need to go out more. Or you need to spend more time alone or with your friends. The goal here is to have no regrets when it's all said and done. So mull over your decision carefully before making any moves. Because once you've parted ways, it's sometimes impossible to get back together.

Breaking Up Is Hard to Do

You've thought it over and you've decided that, yes, definitely your life would be better without him. Now you've just got to figure out how to break the news. I think a face-to-face breakup is best.

SIX SIGNS YOU SHOULD MAKE THE SPLIT

1. You're annoyed—not excited—when you see him.
2. You're dating him because everyone else likes him, not because you like him.
3. He treats you like dirt, and you know it.
4. When he does something sweet for you, you think he's "whipped."
5. You constantly make excuses not to see him.
6. You have a major crush on someone else.

Of course, breaking up by e-mail, letter, or phone is easier, but it's really not the nicest way. If it's the only way you feel you can go through with it, however, you've got to do what you've got to do. Before you do it, put yourself in his shoes. If you can handle an up-close-and-personal encounter, that's the way to go. It's what's likely to give you both the most closure, and saves him face.

I'd always heard that breaking up in a public place—like a restaurant or a mall—is best, because it ensures he won't make too much of a scene. Unfortunately, I found out the hard way that this isn't always the case. I once broke up with a guy at Chili's, and he burst into tears at the table. He then insisted we leave, even though our food hadn't even arrived yet. The lesson? If he's prone to emotional outbursts, a public place isn't the best choice. Otherwise, you'll both feel embarrassed and exposed.

Before you meet him for "the talk," write down what you're going to say. Why exactly are you breaking up with him? If the reasons are too harsh to say out loud (like he's a bad kisser or a complete cheapskate), be kind. Don't annihilate his self-esteem. Just divulge the reasons that won't crush him. Like you feel that you both are just too different. Or he's a bit too jealous and controlling for your taste. Or you don't want to be in a serious relationship right now. Once you write the reasons down and recite them a few times in front of your mirror, you'll feel stronger when it's actually showtime.

Now, once you deliver your speech, it could go a couple of different ways. He could tell you you're wrong and beg you to change your mind. With aforementioned Chili's Man, I actually took him back once because I felt so sorry for him and so bad about making him cry. He promised he'd change. But of course he couldn't change his entire personality, and that was basically the problem. And three weeks later I had to break up with him all over again, and that time it was even worse. So if you are tempted to take him back just because you feel sorry for him, save yourself the agony and don't do it. You've got to put your feelings first, not his. (If you really do want to take him back, however, check out "Getting Back Together" on page 196.)

If he starts crying, listen to him as long as you can, but stick to your guns. He's upset, but he'll get over it. Since you're obviously not meant for each other, you're doing you both a big favor by ending it. Someday he'll realize that. And if he starts yelling or making a scene, leave. If he gets violent, call 911 if you have to. Don't put yourself in a dangerous situation.

What if he wants to "still be friends"? While Jerry and Elaine make it look easy on those Seinfeld reruns, being buds with an ex can be anything but. The acid test: Will you be able to handle it when he talks about his new girlfriend? And would you feel comfortable talking to him about your new boyfriend? If the answer is no, remember that making the transition from girlfriend to just-friend can be a rough one. Take a break from each other and give yourselves some time.

The Morning After

If you go to school with or work with your ex, splitting up with him doesn't exactly provide a clean break. What do you do when you see him in the halls, sit by him at work, or actually have to talk to him? Avoid him when possible, and be cordial but not overly friendly when you have to deal with him. Breaking up with someone is like peeling off a scab. You've got to put a Band-Aid on it and give it time to heal. And it won't heal properly if you're involved in each other's business after the breakup.

If he is being immature or spreading rumors about you, let him know in no uncertain terms that you will not tolerate it. You deserve better than that! But don't stoop to his level. Just because he is being a total idiot doesn't mean you have to be one, too. Be the bigger person. Go on with your life. Because happiness really is the best revenge!

is it time to give him the boot?

1. You're on your way to a party when you develop a splitting headache. What does your boyfriend do?

a) Immediately pulls over to get you some aspirin and water, then asks you if you want to skip the bash

b) Tells you to get over it, then turns up the radio even louder

c) Looks somewhat concerned, then says you can get some aspirin at the party

2. On average, how many fights do you have per week?

a) More than Oscar de la Hoya

b) Three to five

c) Two or less

3. When you're with him, how do you normally feel?

a) Stressed out

b) Happy as a clam

c) Miserable

4. How many times has he blown off one of your dates?

a) Too many to mention

b) Never

c) Once or twice

5. When you're fighting, how does he act?

   a) Sometimes rude and sometimes not-so-rude, depending on his mood

   b) Like a bully—calling you names, screaming, the whole nine

   c) Level-headed—stating his case, listening to yours, keeping his cool

6. Does your guy drink or do drugs on a regular basis?

   a) No

   b) Only on the weekends

   c) Yes

7. What did your man get you for your birthday?

   a) Nothing

   b) A sweet, homemade gift

   c) Dinner for two at Pizza Hut

8. How much do you have in common?

   a) Not much

   b) A ton

   c) Nothing

9. When you picture yourself with another guy, how do you feel?

   a) Happy and free

   b) Scared but excited

   c) Really upset

10. Would your life be better without him?

   a) No

   b) Yes

   c) You're not sure.

11. Why are you still with him?

    a) Because you've been with him so long, you hate to give up now

    b) Because you hope he'll act like he did when you first started dating

    c) Because you love him

Scoring:

1. a) 3; b) 1; c) 2	**6.** a) 3; b) 2; c) 1
2. a) 1; b) 2; c) 3	**7.** a) 1; b) 3; c) 2
3. a) 2; b) 3; c) 1	**8.** a) 2; b) 3; c) 1
4. a) 1; b) 3; c) 2	**9.** a) 1; b) 2; c) 3
5. a) 2; b) 1; c) 3	**10.** a) 3; b) 1; c) 2
	11. a) 2; b) 1; c) 3

Calculate your score to find out if you should kiss him or dis him.

11–17: Ditch Him

There should be no question here. You've got to kick this one to the curb! He treats you like dirt, and you can do so much better. And you can't find anyone better until you throw this loser back. The sooner you make the split, the better.

18–25: Something's Got to Give

He isn't treating you as well as you deserve to be treated, that's a fact. But he's not all bad either. Just when you are ready to show him the door, he does some sweet thing to win you back. But the fact is: You need to see bigger changes than the ones he's made so far. And if he doesn't shape up, you'd be wise to ship him out.

26–33: Hold on Tight

Everyone thinks about breaking up with her guy some of the time, even if he is great. It's natural. But before you throw yours out, take a look at what you've got. He treats you well, is a total sweetheart, and makes you happy. Unless you have zero attraction for him, stick around. He's a diamond in the rough.

chapter 11

decidedly dumped

Y ou've been dumped. And it sucks. Correction: It really, really sucks. Go ahead, go through a box of Kleenex. Or two. Then devour a few pints of Ben & Jerry's. But once the initial ohmigod-I-can't-believe-he-broke-up-with-me shock passes (and it will, believe me), there's going to be some major repair work to do. See, your heart's been broken. Demolished. Smashed. And it's up to you to figure out how to fix it. Here, a step-by-step guide to surviving the split in style.

Taking the News

The second the breakup begins is the second he tells you he wants to end the relationship. It's impossible to articulate the kind of pain you feel at that moment, especially if you never saw it coming. There are a million ways you might react, and none of them is right or wrong. My only bit of advice here is don't beg him to change his mind. If you want to talk, there'll be time for that later. After hearing news such as this, initiating a big talk is a bad idea. You're too upset to think straight. See if he'll agree to meet with you a week later. That way you'll both have time to cool down and think things over. Being broken up with is kind of like being in a car wreck. Only in this case, the car has a gas leak and might blow any minute. It's an emergency situation. Get out as fast as you can.

Rescue 911

Immediately after the breakup, you're going to be a wreck. A zillion questions will run through your mind, the top three being (a) why did he break up with me? (b) how can he live without me? and (c) when is he going to come to his senses? Unfortunately, you may never get the answers to any of the above, so I'll save you some time and answer them for you:

a) He broke up with you because he's an idiot.

b) He can live without you because he's too dense to realize how great of a girl he just let go.

c) He'll probably never come to his senses, so be happy you're free of him sooner rather than later.

That said, let's get to the matter at hand: your broken heart.

First, get on the phone and call all of your best friends. Not the "friends" who are going to pump you for all the details and then spread them all over school or the "pals" who are secretly thrilled you broke up so they can go after your ex themselves. Just call the friends who won't make fun of you for having mascara running down your face or for telling the same sob story a thousand times. Only your true-blue buds will do in a case like this. Tell them to get over to your house immediately, because you need a few shoulders to cry on.

When they arrive, go over every detail of the breakup. Encourage your pals to tell you what a jerk he is. Punch the pillow on your bed and pretend it's his face. Pull out every love note he ever wrote you. Obsess. Freak out. You've got to get these feelings out of your system at some point, and it might as well be now. While you are going berserk, be sure to eat lots of chocolate—but avoid Hershey's Kisses, as anything that has "kisses" in the name is bad. Very bad.

Once you're all talked out, get a picture of your ex out of your wallet or shoe box or whatever (in a pinch, a yearbook photo or stick-figure drawing will do). Then practice how you're going to act when you see him again. Keep in mind: Less is more. If you're smiling and laughing with friends and don't give him as much as a look when you're walking down the hall, suddenly you're the one who got away, not the one still lusting after him. As I've said, happiness is the best revenge. So rehearse your laugh. That carefree flip of your hair over your shoulder. The look that tells him you're over him, even if you aren't. If you do happen to tear up at the sight of him without you, the old "I've got something in my eye" line works like a charm. Because you do have something in your eye—a teardrop. But he doesn't have to know what it is, does he?

Now get some shut-eye. The sooner you go to sleep, the sooner this day can be behind you. And then you'll be one day closer to being over him, which is a very good thing.

The Day After

The first few seconds after you wake up, you'll feel great. Until you remember—you've just been dumped. Then reality will come crashing down upon you like a ton of bricks. Don't worry—things will get better after you physically get up. So drag your butt out of bed and put on your favorite CD (bonus points if it doesn't remind you of him). Even though you probably feel like staying in your sweats and grungy T, force yourself to make an effort here. Doll yourself up. You'll feel a million times better if you look ultra-cute today, and—if it's a school day—those admiring gazes from male classmates won't hurt your ego either.

Breaking the breakup news to your parents is a delicate matter. If you're close, chances are you told them the second he said "See ya." But even if you're not thisclose, go ahead and break the news over breakfast. They probably suspect something's up anyway, given your puffy eyes and newfound penchant for sappy Backstreet Boys songs. Let them know you're upset and could use their support right now, then leave things at that. Dad will probably tell you you're too good for him anyway (you are) and Mom will likely offer to take you shopping that weekend (score!). Depending on how close you are with your siblings, their sympathies will range from heartfelt to nonexistent. Estimate their compassion quotient, then proceed with caution.

School is going to be excruciating—especially the first couple of days. Lean on your friends, throw yourself into your schoolwork, and refuse to talk to him at all costs. If he tells you he wants to "talk," tell him you need at least a week to think things over. Right now, the feelings are too fresh for either one of you to be objective. Don't talk to him face-to-face or accept his calls for at least seven days. And, yes, this means no calling him either. Yikes. What will you do with yourself? For some ideas, see page 190.

The Talk

So you've survived the first week without him. Congrats! Now it's time for the "talk." This conversation may not come to pass

WHAT TO DO INSTEAD OF CALLING HIM

- Write him a letter, but don't send it.
- Take belly-dancing lessons.
- Bond like mad with all your best buds.
- Give yourself and your friends expert manicures and pedicures.
- Catch up with Daria, Buffy, and all your other favorite TV heroines.
- Paint and rearrange your bedroom.
- Buy a poster board, then cover it with every single one of your goals.
- See every movie he refused to see with you.
- Develop a crush on a major cutie.
- Put together at least five new outfits.
- Dye your hair a shocking new color.
- Call all the friends you didn't see much when you were with him.
- Go dancing at an all-ages club.
- Write a short story with you as the fab main character.
- Make a list of every bad thing he ever did to you, then read it when you think you miss him.
- Rent every girl-empowering movie you can think of.
- Have an all-girls sleepover.
- Reread your favorite book of all time.
- Camp out for tickets to see your favorite band (yes, the one he hates!).
- Buy a new shade of lipstick for every day of the week.
- List all your fabulous qualities in your journal.
- Put on a tiara, because you're the queen of the world!

if neither one of you has approached the other—sometimes a clean break is best. If he left you for another girl, for instance, he's not even worth wasting your breath on. But if there are some unresolved issues lurking about, talking them out now could save you thousands on therapy bills down the road. Before you meet up, make a list of things you'd like to talk to him about, phrased in question form. Be as specific as possible. A broad question such as "Why did you break up with me?" might get a mumbled "I dunno," but the more specific "What made you ditch me for your Sega three Fridays in a row?" will probably elicit a more specific response.

Keep in mind that you may not necessarily get the answers you're looking for. As we've covered, girls mature faster than guys. So even if he's a few years older than you, you're probably much more grown-up than he is. The deal is: Most girls analyze things to death, while guys tend to blow things off. You could be completely upset while he's hanging with the guys not thinking a thing about it. Not all guys are this way—thank goodness—but if you've got yourself one of the laid-back variety, chances are he'll never tell you what you want to hear. A boy I was completely in love with wrecked my world, but I never found out for sure exactly why he treated me like crap. In fact, we never really had a heart-to-heart after the fact. So instead of figuring out why he treated me that way, I had to ask myself why I allowed him to treat me this way. And then I could move on. If your guy is MIA, turn the questions you have for him into questions for yourself. For example:

Question for Him: Why didn't you call me that Saturday like you said you would? I waited all day for your call.

Question for You: Why did I wait around all day for a call from someone who doesn't respect me and my time enough to keep his word?

Maybe you liked him so much, you gave him the benefit of the doubt. Or you were scared to be alone. Or you thought all guys were just like that. Once you start asking yourself some of this stuff, you can gain the insight you need to get over him. But don't be surprised if you miss him along the way.

Missing Him

Sometimes you don't miss him as much as you miss the person you wanted him to be. And, of course, the future "us" you had banked upon—the happy couple who was going to go to the prom together and attend the same college and live happily ever after—is now dead in the water as well. But it would be impossible for you to be with a person as much as you were with your ex and NOT miss him. It's like someone came in and stole your favorite pajamas. Of course you'd miss how soft they felt against your skin, the comfort you felt wearing them night after night, that light shade of pink they'd faded to after too many turns in the dryer. But getting some new PJs would be a good thing, too.

You could pick a really cool print or try a different style or fabric. Same thing with guys. You'll miss the old one for a while—it's only natural. But a new one will undoubtedly take his place, and soon you'll have a new favorite. But not before mourning the loss of your old one first.

Depression Confession

On the road to recovery, it's natural to feel down. But if you feel lower than low, you could be clinically depressed. To find out, check out the following warning signs:

- **The Belly Blahs:** People who eat four Reese's candy bars in one sitting or find themselves inhaling an entire large pizza at dinner. Eating more than usual is a big depression warning sign. But if you're not eating much at all, you're not exactly okay either. If your clothes are suddenly too big or you find yourself absolutely stuffed after downing three carrot sticks, this is another red light.
- **The Snooze Blues:** If you're having a hard time sleeping or feel drowsy all the time, there could be some major trouble.
- **The Loner Lows:** Hate hanging with your buds? Want to be alone rather than with other people? Beep, beep, beep—the depression alarm is going off big-time.

Feeling worthless and alone for more than two weeks can also mean you're depressed. When your brain is bummed, it sends you signals for help. Suddenly you might feel like there's no point to going to school anymore, figuring, "I'm not learning anything, so what's the point?" Obviously, this isn't a logical argument—you learn things in school every day, and you have to go to school to get anywhere in life. But when you're depressed, everything you once found worthwhile can suddenly seem stupid or pointless. Your brain is having trouble deciphering what matters and what doesn't. Because of this, you might have trouble concentrating in class. It's hard to focus on things that used to be no problem for you.

Has your outlook on everything—not just guys—taken a nose-dive? Do you have a negative view of yourself, the world around you, and your future? If you feel bad about all of the above, you're definitely depressed. Talk to a school counselor or therapist to deal with your out-of-control feelings, because— when untreated—depression can be very serious. Even deadly.

Not Worth Dying Over

If you feel like you want to end it all, you need to talk to some-

one immediately. Call a friend, a family member, or anyone you trust and tell them what you're going through. If you can't bear to share your pain with someone you know, call a suicide hotline such as the Nine Line at 1-800-999-9999. An understanding coun-

BEEN THERE, DONE THAT

"I tried to kill myself when my boyfriend broke up with me. It was completely stupid of me, but at the time I felt like I didn't want to live. After I swallowed all these sleeping pills, however, I panicked and called an ambulance. I got rushed to the hospital and had my stomach pumped. That was a year ago. Now I have great friends and good grades and a new boyfriend. I can't tell you how grateful I am my plan didn't work. I have everything to live for, and I almost threw it away for a jerk who didn't even visit me in the hospital." —Molly, 14

selor will discuss your situation with you and help you get the assistance you so desperately need. It's absolutely imperative that you call a hotline if you're even thinking about suicide. No guy is worth dying over! Believe me—I know from experience.

A high school acquaintance of mine went berserk when her boyfriend of two years broke up with her. She sank deeper and deeper into depression, but everyone pretty much told her it was "normal" to feel that way. Well, it finally got so bad that she drove to her ex-boyfriend's house, poured lighter fluid all over herself on his front lawn, then set herself on fire. She didn't die, but she did suffer third-degree burns on 90 percent of her body. Her life was never the same, and—even though he was upset— his life went on pretty much business as usual. When she was fighting for her life in the burn unit, he was probably whooping it up with the girl he'd ditched her for. So it is so not worth it!

If you don't want to talk to someone over the phone, you could go to an emergency room or dial 911. Hospitals have mental health professionals on board who can help you through your ordeal. Feel weird about going to a hospital? Even though you might not have a broken leg or ruptured appendix, you do have a genuine life-threatening medical emergency. And nothing is worth killing yourself over. No matter how bad you feel right now, you're going to feel better in the future. Give yourself the chance to prove that statement right.

Getting Back Together

Okay, so you've had the talk, you've given each other some space—and now you're actually thinking of getting back together. Before you jump back into anything, think it over long and hard. Do you like having him as a boyfriend, or do you just like having a boyfriend in general? Sure, he's a surefire date for all the biggies: the spring formal, Thanksgiving at your aunt's, the opening of the latest Matt Damon flick. But are you taking him back because you want a date desperately or because you want him desperately?

If you decide you want him desperately, then by all means give it another shot. If you don't, you'll always wonder "what if" and could still be hung up on him at your tenth high-school reunion. (Drag!) But be sure to lay down some ground rules beforehand. If he did some things you didn't like the first time around, let him know you're not standing for it this time. Or if you didn't communicate very well, vow to talk things over from here on out. And since every partnership is a two-way street, be sure to ask him if there's anything he'd like you to improve upon as well. Discuss how you can better the relationship before diving back into it. Because it already failed once, and unless you both try to fix things, it's bound to fail again.

If you're not so sure you should take him back, then don't. You'll be cheating yourself if you get back together with a guy who doesn't float your boat. What if you get back together with him but then meet the guy of your dreams three days later? By the time you finally break it off with your now on-again guy, Mr. Dreamboat could very well be dating someone else. So you could screw up your chance with a guy you really liked just because you were afraid to be alone.

are you officially over him?

1. You're at the mall when you spot your ex. What do you do?
- a) Sit down immediately—because your knees are shaking so violently, you can't stand up
- b) Walk by him without even batting an eye
- c) Feel sick for a second, then recover quickly enough to shoot him a wave

2. How many times a day do you think about him?
- a) Three to five
- b) More than six
- c) Two or less

3. If I was to quiz your best friend, how many times would she say you talk about your ex in a single day?
- a) Pretty much never
- b) If the subject happens to just naturally come up, you sometimes speak his name.
- c) So many she's thinking about taping your mouth shut

4. An unbelievably hot guy asks you if you want to go out. What's your reply?
- a) "I'd love to!"
- b) "Well, uh, I'm sort of involved with somebody right now."
- c) "Um, could we double-date with my bud and her boyfriend?"

5. Where are all your pictures of your ex?

> a) Still hanging up all over your room
>
> b) In the trash can
>
> c) Stashed in a cardboard box at the top of your closet

6. If your guy is dating again, how do you feel about the chick he's seeing?

> a) She's not your favorite person in the world, but you tolerate her.
>
> b) You hate her, you hate her, you hate her!
>
> c) You feel sorry for her because she's dating such a loser.

7. You're on a first date with someone new. What's the main topic of conversation?

> a) How much you hate your ex, what a jerk he is, and how you hope you never see him again
>
> b) Whatever comes to mind
>
> c) Your respective feelings on love, relationships, and current events

8. When you hear "your song" on the radio, what do you do?

> a) Turn the station immediately
>
> b) Listen to it for a few minutes, then put in a rockin' CD
>
> c) Sing along at the top of your lungs and cry your heart out

Scoring:

1. a) 3; b) 1; c) 2   **5.** a) 3; b) 1; c) 2
2. a) 2; b) 3; c) 1   **6.** a) 2; b) 3; c) 1
3. a) 1; b) 2; c) 3   **7.** a) 3; b) 1; c) 2
4. a) 1; b) 3; c) 2   **8.** a) 1; b) 2; c) 3

Is he ancient history or front-page news? Find out!

8–13: You're so over him, it's not even funny.

In your mind, your ex is ancient history. You don't care what he's doing or who he's doing it with, because you have moved on in a major way. As long as you've dealt with your feelings rather than swept them under the rug, your resilience is right-on. Next!

14–18: You're still kind of into him, but you're getting over it.

Okay, your heart still drops when you hear his name. And when you see him, you feel a tad bit queasy. But you know this is all part of getting over him, and you find that you think of him a little less each day. And someday soon, you're sure you won't think of him at all. You can't wait!

19–24: You're so hung up, you're practically a hanger.

Even though the relationship is

over, you're keeping it alive in your heart. You're still in love with him, and are holding out hope that he'll see the light and come back to you. But it's over. The sooner you accept that, the sooner you can move on. Do you really want to spend the rest of your life waiting around for this jerk? I didn't think so!

chapter 12

life without guys

Sure, this book is all about guys, but I hope by now you know that you don't have to have one to be happy. Contrary to popular belief, being single doesn't suck. In fact, the whole concept of "Single=Loser" was probably started by Valentine's Day card companies and bicycle-built-for-two manufacturers in hopes that everybody would pair up and boost their business. Well, listen up, Hallmark: Single is not only non-pathetic, it's completely kick-ass! Read on to find why flying solo can be totally terrific.

• **You can flirt with whoever you want.**

Say a smoldering boy comes up to you and your attached friend at a bash. While you can do whatever you wish (i.e., check him out, whisper in his ear, get his number), your pal has to behave like a Girl Scout no matter how cute he is. But your solo self can flirt with every guy in the party if you like. Or kiss a foxy fellow just for the hell of it. After all, you're free as a bird!

• You can hang with your friends.

Even though it sucks, a lot of girls ditch their friends for their boyfriends. Lame! Maybe they bail on your weekly Girls' Night or blow you off when their boy beeps in on call-waiting. You, on the other hand, are true blue. Since you're single, you can spend quality time with your chums and really bond your butt off—without guilt trips from some guy.

• You save tons of cash.

Buying gifts for your boy can be extremely expensive. There's his birthday, your three-month anniversary, Valentine's Day, the anniversary of your first kiss . . . you get the picture. All of those celebratory candlelit dinners and beautifully wrapped DVDs can really add up. When you're solo, you can take all that money

 you're saving and treat yourself to a pedicure, a three-month gym membership, or an aromatherapy massage. Go ahead—celebrate your singledom in style!

• You can watch whatever you want without hearing any guy gripes.

You love Drew Barrymore movies. He doesn't. Well, now, who

cares what he does or doesn't like? You get to
see whatever your heart desires. And you're
free to watch your favorite TV shows without
enduring a bored boyfriend begging you to

turn it to ESPN. Best of all, you are the sole master of the
remote, and any channel surfing you do is on your terms.

• **Your time is yours and yours alone.**
When you're someone's girlfriend, you spend a lot of time doing
things for him—you know, that whole give-and-take thing. But
since you're a solo unit, you don't have to worry about things
like helping him with his Trig homework or baby-sitting his little
brother. You do whatever you want, whenever you want!

• **You can hang all the cute-boy posters you desire.**
Some guys go crazy when you salivate over your cute-boy pin-
ups—as if you might just run off with the celeb any minute and
leave him in the lurch. But without Mr. Insecure hovering over
your shoulder, you can feast your eyes on any poster you like
without hearing his snide remarks or discovering a markered-in
mustache over Leo's lip.

• **You can dress however you please.**
If you're hot and heavy with a guy, you might be tempted to
wear those skintight pants he's so into or slip into the six-inch
heels that elevate you to a more suitable kissing level. As a sin-

gle girl, however, you dress solely to impress yourself—and feel seriously stylish as a result!

• You can have a major crush.

You know how when you're dating someone you sometimes meet a guy you would totally go for if you weren't already attached? Well, when you're solo, you can dive headfirst into your killer crush without any fear of repercussions!

• When your friends are griping about their boyfriends, your lips are sealed.

A girlfriend rants every once in a while—about her boyfriend's ugly new high-tops, the way he ditched her at the last minute for his friends, how he hasn't called in three days. But you can remain terrifically tight-lipped (and stress-free) during their bitch sessions. Such a carefree feeling!

• Your possibilities are endless.

Dreaming of going to college in another country? Feel like vegging in front of the tube and giving yourself a facial instead of going out on a Saturday night? Want to fill your little black book to capacity? Whatever your heart desires, you can make it happen—without having to worry about stepping on anyone's toes.

• You don't have to compromise.

He wants to go to a party, you want to go to play miniature golf. Who wins? When you're single, you prevail every time. The only needs you have to pacify are your own!

• You can concentrate on what *you* really want.

When you're going out with someone, it's easy to concentrate so much on his needs that you overlook your own. But when you're solo, you can spend hours upon hours figuring out exactly what you want out of life and how you're going to get it.

are you solo material?

1. The homecoming dance is next week and you don't have a date lined up. What do you do?

    a) Go ahead and go with your friends

    b) Stay home—no way are you showing up without a date!

    c) Talk a guy friend into going with you

2. One of your pals is throwing an all-girls slumber party. Will you be there?

    a) You'll drop by for a little while, then go somewhere more exciting later.

    b) Wouldn't miss it for the world!

    c) No way—a guy-free evening sounds like one big bore.

3. You have plans with your best girlfriend. Five minutes before you're going to leave, a guy calls asking you out for that very evening. You:

    a) call your friend and cancel.

    b) tell him you already have plans, but ask if you can take a raincheck.

    c) tell him you'll call him right back, then call your chum and see what she thinks you should do.

4. It's Saturday night, and you're utterly dateless. You:

    a) call a friend and commiserate about being single for a while, then head over to Blockbuster.

    b) sit around moping the entire evening, feeling like a big, fat loser.

    c) do exactly what you want to do—take a bubble bath, listen to your favorite CDs, paint your toenails.

5. When you are boyfriend-less, you feel like:

    a) a pathetic and ugly failure.

    b) you're a free agent.

    c) the right one is bound to come along someday.

6. What are your favorite kind of songs?

    a) Sappy love songs

    b) Anything you can dance to

    c) Songs with a message

7. What's your top priority right now?

    a) Concentrating on school

    b) Hanging with your friends

    c) Finding a boyfriend

8. Fill in the blank: If I had a boyfriend right now, my life would be:

    a) a tad more intriguing.

    b) just as cool as it is now.

    c) perfect!

Does singledom make you feel stressed or blessed? Read on.

8–13: Seriously Single and Loves to Mingle

When you're single, you don't sulk—you celebrate! You definitely don't need a guy to make you happy. If the right one came along, you wouldn't refuse him—but you're perfectly okay on your own. Continue to live life to the fullest, and you'll have no regrets.

14–19: Somewhere in the Middle

One minute you're super-excited about being single; the next, you're welling up at a mushy love scene, wishing you had someone to smooch. How badly you want a boyfriend largely depends on what night of the week it is. Don't worry: Mood swings are normal, especially when it comes to love. Just go with the flow.

20–24: Looking for Love

In your eyes, life without love is practically not worth living. How are you supposed to have any fun if you don't have someone to go out with on Saturday nights or hold your hand during scary movies? Let me let you in on a little secret: A boyfriend is cool and all—but he should be the icing on the cake, not the entire cake. You've got to be happy with life without a boyfriend before you can be happy with life with one!

conclusion

So there you have it, every single thing I know about guys—at least for right now. Because I learn something new every day. And I'm sure you will, too. Just remember, don't put up with anyone's crap! Because, as I've said a million times, you deserve better than that. You're the coolest. You deserve a cool boyfriend. And until you find one cool enough, being solo is totally okay! I hope what I've shared will help you seek out boys who are worthy of someone like you and dump the ones who aren't. Please e-mail me your questions or comments at GuysExpert@aol.com. Can't wait to hear about all your new-and-improved dating adventures.

You rule!

Love, Julie

index

A

abuse. *See* bad behavior
age gap, 78
AIDS. *See* HIV/AIDS
airport observation deck date, 85
alcohol use, 97-99, 101
Anarchist, The, 21-22, 37
anger, dealing with, 148-52
arguments, 150-52
asking out, 74-77
    by girl, 74-76
    by guy, 76-77
athletic type, 29-30, 38-39

B

bad behavior, 91-111, 197
    blow off as, 92-93
    breaking up because of, 106
    cheating as, 95-96
    date rape as, 99-101
    dealing with, 101, 102-6
    emotional abuse as, 101-3
    lying as, 93-95
    physical abuse as, 104-5
    quiz, 108-11
    reasons for acceptance of,
      107-8
    refusing to accept, 102-3, 104

    stalking as, 105-6
    substance abuse as, 97-99
Best Bud, The, 19-21, 38
"biggie" dates, 85-86
bingo game date, 82
birth control, 134-36, 145
    and STD protection, 133, 134
    types of, 135
black sheep type, 37
blind dates, 77
blow off, 92-93
Brainiac, The, 18-19, 39
break up, 175-201
    because of bad behavior, 106
    being dumped, 185-201
    dealing with, 188-93
    depression warning signs,
      193-94
    getting back together, 196-97
    initiating, 175-83
    quizes on, 180-83, 198-201
    six signs of, 177
    suicidal thoughts, 194-96
    See also single life

C

casual sex, 116-17
celebrity crush, 43-44
cervical cap, 135

National Gay and Lesbian Hotline, 48
Nine Line, The (suicide hot line), 194
Norplant, 135
note passing, 152, 153

O

obscene e-mail, 165
obsessive crushes, 46-47
    and stalking, 105-6
older guys
    crushes on, 45-46
    dating, 78
online relationships. See cyber relationship
oral contraceptive, 135
oral sex, 132-33
orgasm, 130, 137-38

P

Partier, The, 32-33, 37
partying, 207
    drinking or drugging and, 97-98
    as guy type, 32-33, 37
    and sexual activity, 139-40
penis, 132
period, menstrual, 136
phoning. See telephone use
physical abuse, 104-5
physical sex. See sex
pickup lines, 59-62
Pill, The, 135
planetatrium visits, 82
Poet, The, 27-29, 36-37
politican type, 22-24, 38

precautions
    against abusive relationship, 102-3, 104
    against date rape, 100-101
    against date's drinking or drugging, 98
    in cyber relationship, 164-65, 167-69
pregnancy, 134, 136. See also birth control
Prom date, 85-86

Q

quizes
    bad behavior, 108-11
    break up, 180-83, 198-201
    commitment, 124-27
    communication rating, 154-57
    crush, 50-53
    dream date, 34-39
    flirting, 68-71
    long-distance love, 171-73
    physical sex, 142-45
    second-date material, 87-89
    single life, 208-11

R

rape, 140-41
    as cyber relationship risk, 165
    by date, 99-101
Rape, Abuse, and Incest National Network (RAINN), 100
role-playing, 149-50
rotating dinner date, 83